AF245598

LABOUR AND DEVELOPMENT IN RURAL CUBA

LABOUR AND DEVELOPMENT IN RURAL CUBA

Dharam Ghai
Chief of the Rural Employment Policies Branch
Employment and Development Department
International Labour Office

Cristóbal Kay
Lecturer, Department of Political Economy
University of Glasgow

and

Peter Peek
Senior Economist
Rural Employment Policies Branch
International Labour Office

A study prepared for the International Labour Office within the framework of the World Employment Programme

St. Martin's Press   New York

All rights reserved. For information, write:
Scholarly & Reference Division,
St. Martin's Press, Inc., 175 Fifth Avenue, New York, NY 10010

First published in the United States of America in 1988

Printed in Hong Kong

ISBN 0–312–00982–8

Library of Congress Cataloging-in-Publication Data
Ghai, Dharam P.
Labour and development in rural Cuba.
Bibliography: p.
Includes index.
1. Manpower policy, Rural—Cuba.   2. Agriculture—
Economic aspects—Cuba.   3. Rural development—Cuba.
4. State farms—Cuba.   5. Agriculture, Cooperative—
Cuba.   6. Cuba—Rural conditions.   I. Kay, Cristóbal.
II. Peek, Peter.   III. Title.
HD5741.A6G48   1988   331.11′097291   87–13137
ISBN 0–312–00982–8

The World Employment Programme (WEP) was launched by the International Labour Organisation in 1969, as the ILO's main contribution to the International Development Strategy for the Second United Nations Development Decade.

The means of action adopted by the WEP have included the following:
— short-term high-level advisory missions:
— longer-term national or regional employment teams; and
— a wide-ranging research programme.

Through these activities the ILO has been able to help national decision-makers to reshape their policies and plans with the aim of eradicating mass poverty and unemployment.

A landmark in the development of the WEP was the World Employment Conference of 1976, which proclaimed *inter alia* that 'strategies and national development plans should include as a priority objective the promotion of employment and the satisfaction of the basic needs of each country's population'. The Declaration of Principles and Programme of Action adopted by the Conference will remain the cornerstone of WEP technical assistance and research activities during the 1980s.

This publication is the outcome of a WEP project.

Contents

List of Tables

List of Figures

Preface

This study forms part of the ongoing research undertaken within the framework of the World Employment Programme of the ILO. The basic objective of this research is to contribute to the solution of employment and poverty problems, particularly in developing countries. The rural component has comprised studies on poverty, alternative agrarian systems, access to food, women workers, organisations of the rural poor, participation, migration and labour markets. The present study on the living standards and work patterns of labour in rural Cuba, part of a series of case studies, touches on several of these themes. It is based on a three-week field visit to Cuba made by the authors in February 1985.

The study could not have been undertaken without a great deal of help from many institutions and individuals. Our greatest debt is to the State Committee on Labour and Social Security (CETSS) in Cuba for authorisation to undertake the study and for making the arrangements for our field visits and discussions. We are also grateful to the Ministry of Agriculture (MINAG), the Ministry of Sugar (MINAZ) and the National Association of Small Farmers (ANAP) for assisting in these arrangements. We also received a good deal of help from the State Planning Board (JUCEPLAN) and the State Statistical Office (CEE). In addition, for sharing information and views with us, we extend our thanks to the cooperatives and state farms we visited, as well as research institutes, local authorities, Communist Party organs, the Cuban Workers' Confederation (CTC) and the enterprise-based unions.

It is not possible to mention by name all the individuals who assisted us in Cuba. However, we would like to record our deep appreciation to the following officials who were especially helpful: Alfredo Díaz Urbay, Julio López Iniesta, Lupo Núñez Rodríguez and Ernesto Ramos García.

We were fortunate to receive extensive comments on a preliminary draft of the study from the Cuban authorities, as well as a number of specialists on Cuba and ILO colleagues. Brian Pollitt was especially generous with extremely detailed comments on draft chapters. We also received helpful comments from C. Brundenius, A. Ghose, E. Klein, G. Standing, S. Radwan, M. Hopkins, G. Van Liemt, J. C. Bossio and C. Vasquez.

We are heavily indebted to Noll Scott for an extensive rewrite of the original manuscript. This resulted in major stylistic and substantive improvements as well as considerable shortening of the text. We would like to thank Mr J. P. Martin, Director, Employment and Development Department, for his support throughout the preparation of this study. Mrs E. Schaad helped track down numerous documents and references. Ms S. Deacon and Ms Jouve typed successive drafts of the study. Finally, we are grateful to the Swedish Agency for Research Cooperation with Developing Countries (SAREC) for financing travel and related costs.

DHARAM GHAI
CRISTÓBAL KAY
PETER PEEK

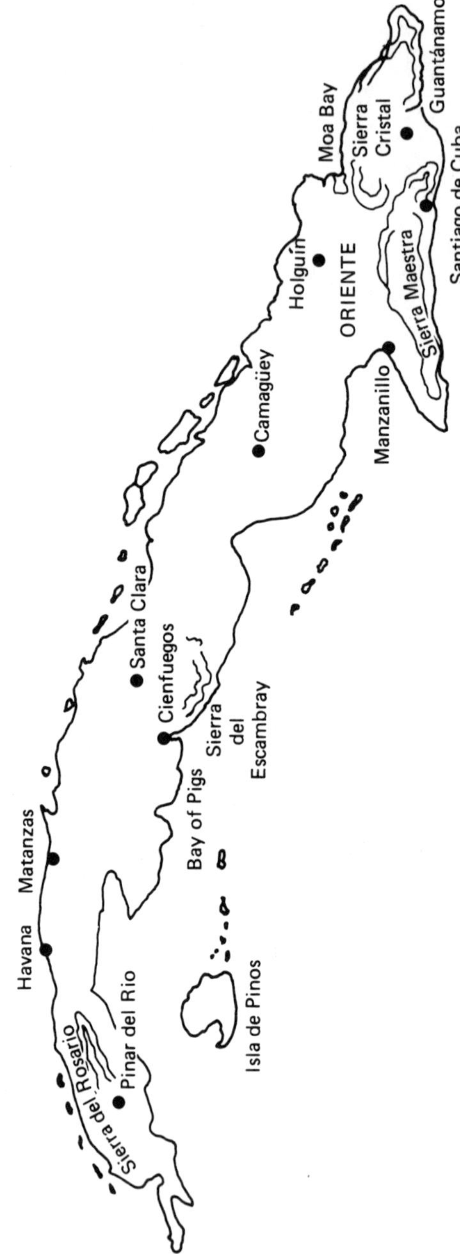

CUBA
Havana
Matanzas
Pinar del Rio
Sierra del Rosario
Santa Clara
Cienfuegos
Bay of Pigs
Sierra del Escambray
Isla de Pinos
Camagüey
Holguín
ORIENTE
Manzanillo
Sierra Maestra
Moa Bay
Sierra Cristal
Guantánamo
Santiago de Cuba

1 Introduction

Cuba's experience of development is of exceptional interest from several points of view. The only socialist country in the western hemisphere, it has now experienced planned development for more than a quarter of a century. Thus sufficient time has elapsed since the 1959 revolution for the country to overcome the problems of transition to a new institutional framework as well as clarify the longer term features of its development approach. There is agreement among commentators of widely divergent backgrounds that the country has achieved a substantial measure of success in generating employment, eliminating poverty and satisfying basic needs. These achievements have been accompanied by impressive economic growth and a highly egalitarian distribution of income and consumption.

The Cuban experience has thus understandably attracted a good deal of attention among students of development. However, while there are several publications dealing with overall development planning and strategy and macroeconomic and social performance, the literature is relatively scarce on rural development. Certainly, there are few recent publications on rural institutions, work patterns and living conditions of peasants and rural workers. Since the early 1970s, a number of significant changes have taken place both in the institutional framework and in mechanisms and policy instruments to regulate economic activities. This study is intended to help fill this gap by focusing on the work and living standards of rural workers and the institutional framework for organising production, emphasising the changes that have taken place since the 1970s.

Most of the material was gathered in the course of a three-week visit to Cuba in February 1985. The most important source of information was the visits paid by the authors to state and cooperative farms, local government organs, educational and health facilities and housing projects. We visited eight state farms and five production cooperatives located in various provinces of the western part of Cuba. One of the authors had earlier visited production and service cooperatives in the eastern part of Cuba.

Of the eight state farms, three specialised in sugar production and two in livestock, while the rest produced a variety of food crops and fruit. Similarly two production cooperatives were involved primarily in sugar cultivation, while others were engaged in cultivating tobacco and food crops. Although the state farms and cooperatives ranged in size and level of development, they cannot be regarded as a representative sample of agricultural enterprises in the country.

The visits to farms, sugar factories, agricultural research institutes, schools, clinics and housing estates not only afforded an opportunity to observe at first hand the work and living standards of the rural population but also to see the working of institutions and policies. Extensive discussions were held with a broad strata of rural society: managers and administrators, teachers and pupils, doctors and nurses, factory and farm workers, private farmers, leaders of cooperatives, local government officials and representatives of central ministries, the Communist Party, the trade unions and the Small Farmers Association (ANAP).

The field visits were followed by discussions in Havana with officials in the State Committee on Labour and Social Security, the State Planning Board, the Ministries of Agriculture and Sugar, the Statistics Bureau, the research institutes, the trade unions and the Small Farmers' Association. Apart from discussions on the broad policy framework and clarification of many detailed points, these visits gave us access to unpublished data, reports and official documents.

In addition to these source materials, we have relied extensively on published literature and the official data on the Cuban economy from various issues of the Statistical Yearbook (*Anuario Estadístico*).

Nevertheless, the reader should be aware of the serious deficiencies in the data which confront those who research the turbulent years of the Cuban revolution, with patchy statistics as far as many topics of great interest are concerned, and a tendency for the basis of calculation to change from one period to another, making it hard to draw firm comparisons.

We have relied for the most part on official data but where alternative sources are available they have been included or what appear to be the most reasonable estimates have been employed. In a book addressed primarily to the general reader it was not felt desirable to dwell at length on each occasion on questions of statistical methodology and detailed discussions of reliability. However, the footnotes refer to specialised publications where such issues are addressed in greater detail.

This study deals primarily with policies and performance in rural employment and the institutional framework for organising rural production in Cuba, emphasising the changes that have occurred since 1970. Chapter 2 provides background information on the structure of agriculture prior to the revolution and the key institutional changes that were made in the first decade after the revolution. There is also a discussion of some important issues of strategy and policy as well as a brief assessment of performance with respect to employment, income distribution and living standards. This is followed, in the next chapter, by an analysis of the main features of the economic reforms launched in the post-1970 period. The purpose of the reforms was to step up economic growth through emphasis on efficiency in resource allocation and use. The main instruments were greater reliance on economic calculus at the enterprise level, decentralisation in planning and management and incentives to managers and workers for increased productivity and more efficient use of resources. Thus Chapter 3 contains a discussion of the key elements of the new Economic Management and Planning System, of wage reforms and incentive schemes, as well as of changes in the pricing, marketing and distribution mechanisms. The following two chapters deal with the three principal modes of agricultural production in Cuba – the state farms, cooperatives and private farming. Among the topics discussed are the organisation of work, methods of remuneration and worker participation in production and management.

Following the examination of institutions and policies, Chapter 6 is devoted to an assessment of social and economic performance since 1970. It deals with social developments such as health, education, housing and economic security; changes in population, labour force and employment; trends in income distribution, overall growth and agricultural performance. The final chapter highlights some distinctive features of the Cuban experience in rural development and draws attention to some underlying weaknesses in the economy and emerging policy issues for the future.

When the work on this book was already completed, the Cuban Government announced in mid-1986 the modification of several key policies. Private farmers' markets were abolished, material incentives became less important and decentralisation was reduced. It has not been possible to take account of these changes in this work. It seems unlikely that these changes represent fundamental reversals of the economic reforms discussed in this book. They should perhaps best be seen as responses to the economic difficulties encountered by the country since late 1985.

2 The First Decade

2.1 AGRICULTURE BEFORE THE REVOLUTION

Although just over half the population lived in urban centres by 1959, Cuba before the revolution was an eminently agrarian country.

Agriculture as such accounted for about a quarter of national income and employed some 40 per cent of the workforce. But the most important branches of industry were also firmly rooted in farming.[1]

Sugar in particular, whose production straddles both industry and agriculture, overshadowed the economy to an impressive and indeed unwelcome degree, accounting for about 80 per cent of the value of exports and more than a quarter of national income.[2] On the ups and downs of international sugar prices and domestic production levels hung the well-being of the economy at large.

An agrarian economy, then. But Cuba's was not a peasant society. Of the rural workforce as a whole, fully 60.6 per cent were wage labourers (see Table 2.1) – the overwhelming majority of them seasonal labourers who sought employment as cane-cutters during the sugar harvest or *zafra*.[3] Within Latin America only Chile had a higher proportion of wage labourers among its rural workforce at the time. And many of those classed as urban industrial workers – the labour force of the sugar mills – actually lived in small semi-rural company towns (*bateyes*) where the production demands of their trade ensured lifelong proximity to the countryside.

Yet the degree of 'proletarianisation' should not be overstated. It has been pointed out that a significant proportion of those classified as agricultural wage-workers in Table 2.1 had access to a plot of land.[4] These plots rarely exceeded 2 hectares and were typically between 0.25 and 1 hectare. To reflect the ambiguity of their class status, such wage-workers have been described as 'semi-proletarians' or alternatively 'semi-peasants'. Although this qualification applied to some extent to many other Third World countries, the incidence of wage labour in the pre-revolutionary Cuban countryside was quite unusually high.

TABLE 2.1   *Rural employment, 1953 (thousands)*

	Men	Women[1]	total	%
Farmers and livestock breeders	220.5	1.5	221.9	27.5
farmers	216.5	1.4	217.9	
livestock breeders	4.0	0.0	4.0	
Agricultural workers	554.9	10.1	564.9	70.0
administrators, foremen	8.8	0.4	9.2	1.1
wage workers	480.5	8.5	489.0	60.6
unwaged family labour[2]	65.5	1.2	66.7	8.3
Others[3]	20.3	0.3	20.7	2.5
Total	795.7	11.8	807.5	100.0

[1] Figures in this column are prone to be a gross underestimate. The census results reflect only the 'primary' occupation. Many women who were active for part of the year were registered as 'housewives'.
[2] Refers generally to the offspring of peasant farmers employed on land rented or owned by their fathers.
[3] Fishermen, hunters, trappers, forestry workers, gardeners.

SOURCE   Comité Estatal de Estadísticas (CEE) *Censos de Población, Viviendas y Electoral*, Havana 1953, table 54, p. 204. Adapted from B. H. Pollitt, 'The transition to socialist agriculture in Cuba: some salient features', in *Bulletin (IDS)* (Sussex, United Kingdom), vol. 13, no. 4, 1982, p. 13.

Another striking feature of the rural scene, though one that was less singular to Cuba, was the endemic un- and underemployment. While a highly unequal pattern of land distribution, exacerbated by a rapid population growth of 2.3 per cent per annum, forced ever-growing numbers on to the labour market, the strong seasonal variations in the demand for labour, imposed by the sugar cycle, meant that the majority of rural workers faced unemployment during the 'dead season' (*tiempo muerto*). In the 1956–7 season, 8–11 per cent of the workforce was idle at any given point during the peak of the *zafra*, rising to 15–21 per cent during the slack season for an overall average of 16.4 per cent.[5] Add to this a further estimated 13.8 per cent underemployed and we see that nearly one-third were partially or wholly jobless.[6]

2.1.1 Land ownership

Land ownership was extremely concentrated. In 1945, the date of the last agricultural census before the revolution (Table 2.2), the large landlords accounted for only 2.8 per cent of all farms, yet their holdings amounted to 57 per cent of the total. At the other end of the

TABLE 2.2   *Land distribution in Cuba, 1945*

	No. of farms	%	Total area[1]	%
Up to 2 caballerías[2]	125 619	78.5	1 362.5	15.0
From 2 to 5 *caballerías*	16 766	10.5	822.5	9.0
From 5 to 30 *caballerías*	13 150	8.2	1 728.2	19.0
Over 30 *caballerías*	4 423	2.8	5 163.8	57.0
Total	159 958	100.0	9 077.0	100.0

[1] Thousands of hectares
[2] Conversions: 2 *caballerías* = 26.8 ha.; 5 *caballerías* = 67.1 ha.; 30 *caballerías* = 402.6 ha.

SOURCE   República de Cuba, *Censo Agrícola Nacional de 1945* (Havana, 1946).

scale, small farmers operated 78.5 per cent of all farms but their land was only 15 per cent of the total. Most of the farm area comprised vast sugar plantations or cattle ranches, and just twenty-two companies (thirteen of them foreign owned) controlled fully 70 per cent of the land under sugar cane, the equivalent of one-fifth of total agricultural land.[7]

Only 36 per cent of farms were operated either directly by their owners, or by administrators working on their behalf. But such holdings comprised 58 per cent of the land. The rest were properties leased out to tenants (*arrendatarios*) and sub-tenants (*subarrendatarios*) for cash, or to sharecroppers (*partidarios*) – typically tobacco farmers[8] – for payment in kind. Squatters (*precaristas*) naturally had no land title of any kind, nor paid any rent.

Table 2.3 shows that the largest farms tended to be those run by administrators, averaging some 248 hectares. These would typically have been cattle estates, the property of absentee landlords. What seems surprising, in view of the concentrated ownership of the giant sugar plantations, is that owner-operated farms should have averaged only 60.6 hectares. The fact is, the owners of the large sugar plantations rarely produced over 30 per cent of the cane their mills consumed, and often substantially less.[9] This cane grown directly by the mills, using hired wage labour, was referred to as 'administration cane'. The rest was produced by tenant farmers known as *colonos* on land rented for cash from the owners.

During the 1930s the *colonos* had achieved security of tenure and rent regulation which gave them some legal protection from abuse by the plantation owners. Despite this, the great mass of *colonos* remained highly vulnerable to the dramatic shifts in production quotas

TABLE 2.3　*Who operated the farms, 1945. Type of operator*

	Number	% of total	Average area[1]	% of total
Owners	48 792	30.5	60.6	32.4
Administrators	9 342	5.8	248.4	25.6
Tenant farmers	46 048	28.8	58.9	30.6
Sub-tenants	6 987	4.4	30.8	2.4
Sharecroppers	33 064	20.7	16.7	6.1
Squatters	13 718	8.6	17.8	2.7
Other	2 007	1.2	35.9	0.8
Total	159 958	100.0	56.7 ha.	100.0

[1] Hectares

SOURCE　República de Cuba, *Censo Agrícola Nacional de 1945* (Havana, 1946).

and procurement prices which the sugar companies imposed on them in response to the fluctuations in international sugar trade. The majority were small farmers who cultivated the land relying mainly on their own family labour. The big *colonos*, on the other hand, did not themselves work the land, but were capitalist tenant farmers and in some cases landowners as well, whose livelihood depended on employed wage labour. The latters' output was a crucial source of raw cane for the mills. In the 1951 harvest, for instance, just 3.9 per cent of the *colonos* produced 56.1 per cent of all cane not produced by the sugar mills.[10]

2.1.2　Production

What the farm sector produced was mostly for export. In 1945, sugar netted 41.6 per cent of total farm income, tobacco 10.2 per cent and coffee 2.7 per cent. Livestock, mainly beef, represented a further 20.9 per cent. But production of staple foods was comparatively neglected, with cereals and beans, root crops, fruit and green vegetables totalling just 19 per cent, which helps to explain why food purchases accounted for such a large proportion – roughly a quarter – of the pre-revolutionary import bill.[11]

2.2　AGRARIAN REFORM

On winning power in 1959 the revolutionary leaders considered that, to escape from underdevelopment, Cuba's historic dependence on sugar had to be confronted directly, and they opted for a strategy of agricultural diversification. The key was to be found, it was thought, in a far-reaching programme of agrarian reform.

Political and social as much as economic criteria lay behind the programme. The redistribution of land to the peasants had long been a central plank of the revolutionary platform. Indeed, Law No. 3 of the guerrilla movement led by Fidel Castro in the mountains of the Sierra Maestra had already anticipated such measures in the areas under rebel control, a few months before the overthrow of the Batista regime.

But in terms of economic strategy, too, the agrarian reform was seen as a basic foundation for securing the new priorities. Not only was the redistribution of land expected to go hand in hand with the diversification of agriculture, but it was also to be a pillar of the industrialisation drive, aimed at the wide-scale substitution of imports through local production. Increased food production would free foreign exchange for investments, it was anticipated, while the enhanced incomes of the peasantry would also help fuel industrial expansion, by increasing demand for the output of the manufacturing sector.

2.2.1 The First Agrarian Reform

The First Agrarian Reform Law was promulgated in May 1959, five months after the revolutionary takeover. Its aim was to expropriate the biggest landlords – defined as those owning over 30 *caballerías* (403 hectares) – and to give full title to smallholders who were cultivating their land under the various tenure arrangements or as squatters.

Most estates and plantations were expropriated outright – if their owners left the country – or reduced to the new upper limits. But those which were managed efficiently, and a number of livestock farms, were allowed to retain up to 100 *caballerías* (1342 hectares). The tenant farmers and squatters, meanwhile, were to be given, free, what was deemed the 'vital minimum' of 2 *caballerías* (26.8 hectares). If they were already cultivating more than this area, they could purchase the rest up to a top limit of 5 *caballerías* (67.1 hectares). Expropriated landowners were to be compensated according to the declared taxable value of their properties, although in the event few received such compensation because they mostly left the country, and nor for that matter did most peasant farmers who received more than 2 *caballerías* ever pay for it.[12]

TABLE 2.4 *The redistribution of land, 1959–63*

	Area (thousands of hectares)	%
Total private land January 1959	*10 070*	*100.0*
Total land expropriated July 1963	*6 073*	*60.3*
Distributed to:		
A. Small peasants	883	8.8
B. The public sector	3 768	37.4
Cane farms	904	
People's Farms	2 844	
Cooperatives	20	
C. State owned lands operated by		
former private manager[1]	1 422	14.1
Land not expropriated[1]	*3 997*	*39.7*

[1] These figures were obtained as residuals.

SOURCE Adapted from A. MacEwan, *Revolution and economic development in Cuba* (London: Macmillan, 1981) pp. 45–6.

The 1959 measures affected about 60 per cent of the land, as Table 2.4 shows. By 1963, the date of the Second Agrarian Reform Law, approximately one-tenth of former owners had been affected. Already by the end of 1961, little more than eighteen months after the agrarian reform was launched, from 3597 farms with more than 30 *caballerías*, accounting between them for 57.3 per cent of Cuban farmland, there survived only 600 such farms, totalling 3.7 per cent of the land.[13]

The medium-sized farms, between 5 and 30 *caballerías*, still represented between one-fifth and one-quarter of the total land and accounted for about half the area remaining under private ownership. This important social force, amounting to an estimated 10 000 capitalist farmers, was thus the only sector to survive – at least for the time being – comparatively unaffected as the large landowners virtually disappeared and the small farmers multiplied.

There were numerous beneficiaries. Between 100 000 and 120 000 tenant farmers, sharecroppers and squatters received ownership titles,[14] bringing the total number of peasant farmers to approximately 150 000.[15] But while the previous average size of peasant smallholdings had been around 35 hectares, the new average of 16 hectares was well under the declared 'vital minimum' of 27 hectares.[16]

2.2.2 The birth of the state farms

The Government apparently never contemplated dividing up the huge landed estates and redistributing them to the peasantry. The outstanding beneficiary of the First Agrarian Reform Law in terms of area was therefore the State itself, and the newly created public farm sector absorbed slightly over half the total farmland (51.5 per cent) as a result.[17] How was this land to be exploited?

The agrarian reform law anticipated in general terms the creation of some form of agrarian cooperatives. In the event, what emerged, with strong official support, were collectives that were more akin to state farms, since the National Institute of Agrarian Reform (INRA – *Instituto Nacional de Reforma Agraria*) appointed the manager and was responsible for financing the new enterprises. After the first year of the reform programme 791 agricultural and livestock cooperatives had been established,[18] and by the end of 1960, 622 cane cooperatives had also been set up[19] federated in 46 Groupings of Cane Cooperatives (*Agrupaciones de Cooperatives Cañeras*), each associated with a particular sugar mill. These cane cooperatives had their own constitutions governing their internal functioning but were also in practice state farms, responding to the directives of INRA. Finally, the large cattle ranches that had been expropriated were taken under the direct control of INRA and were known as Direct Administration Farms (*Fincas de Administración Directa*). Some 500 of these were constituted in the first year of the reform.[20]

2.2.3 The abolition of seasonal labour

For the workers who had previously been permanent employees of the estates, the expropriation of their employers meant that they automatically qualified as permanent members of the new cooperatives. But former seasonal labourers continued to be hired on a seasonal basis. However, when in April 1961 the Government openly proclaimed the socialist character of the revolution, one of whose chief tenets was to be the abolition of 'exploitation of man by man', most of the cooperatives were rapidly transformed into fully fledged state farms, known as People's Farms (*Granjas del Pueblo*), and seasonal workers were taken on with guarantees of full-time employment. Only the cane cooperatives retained their formal status a little longer, until 1962, when they became simply Cane Farms (*Granjas Cañeras*).

The most immediate result of the transformation of the old estates into state farms, passing rapidly through the transitional stage of cooperativisation, was thus the abolition of the scourge of casual seasonal labour – fulfilling a long-standing ambition of the farmworkers themselves. But the move also tied in with the new Government's wider strategic vision. Inevitably, there existed significant disparities between the different farm units, depending on the fertility of their soils or their ease of access to inputs. A relatively autonomous form of cooperative agriculture might, it was feared, compound such differences and lead to a polarisation between rich and poor enterprises. Such a trend would effectively reassert the disadvantages of the remote areas which the revolution had set itself to redress. With all the larger units firmly under state control, on the other hand, the State itself, through INRA, could ensure that resources were redistributed in accordance with the political and social priorities of the moment. In short, as in other areas of the economy, the leadership strongly believed in the social, political and ultimately economic superiority of direct state management over all other forms of production.

2.2.4 Collectivisation and mutualism

With little encouragement from above, meanwhile, a number of peasants had spontaneously formed themselves into collectives after the revolution, and by 1962 there were a total of 358 Agricultural and Livestock Societies (*Sociedades Agropecuarias*). Typically, membership of these collectives would range between twelve and sixteen, while their joint holding would amount to 110 to 160 hectares.[21]

Later, in the mid-1970s, collectives on these lines were to be strongly promoted as a 'socialist form of agriculture'. The structure and role of the *Sociedades* anticipated in most respects the Agricultural Production Cooperatives or CPAs (*Cooperativas de Producción Agropecuaria*) which today dominate the non-state sector. At the time, however, only the state farms were regarded as a 'superior' form and the peasant collectives subsequently tended to disintegrate or merge into the state farms, so that by 1975 only forty-three survived.

Credit and Service Cooperatives or CCSs (*Cooperativas de Créditos y Servicios*), on the other hand, a more restricted form of mutual support, were more strongly encouraged from the outset as a way to channel credit and inputs to individual private farmers. By 1961 there were already some 300 of these in existence, and their numbers continued to expand.[22] Private farmers also frequently combined in mutual aid brigades to help each other with the harvesting.

2.2.5   The Agrarian Reform Institute (INRA)

In their public statements and by their actions, the new authorities particularly sought to emphasise the egalitarian nature of the revolution they were leading. The real army of the poor was to be found in the Cuban countryside,[23] and it was there that the first great changes were principally directed. The early 1960s were also, for instance, the time of the national literacy crusade, in which thousands of pupils and students, mostly from the cities and towns, were dispatched to bring remote communities the skills of reading and writing. The government leadership, fresh from its guerrilla campaign in the mountains of the Sierra Maestra, fought an equally tenacious propaganda battle against the city's traditional contempt for the Cuban *guajiro* (peasant). In 1959, Havana was mobilised to open its homes to tens of thousands of *guajiros* who descended with their *machetes* and straw hats on the capital city, most of them for the first time in their lives, to take part in the first of the annual 26 July celebrations.

Symbolism apart, the central role of rural change and agrarian reform within the overall development of Cuban policy-making in these early years is perhaps best illustrated by the role of INRA, whose early responsibilities came to extend so deeply into industry and other sectors of the economy and society that by the end of 1959 it could be described as the real seat of economic power with the Commander in Chief of the Revolution, Prime Minister Fidel Castro, at its head. From INRA can be traced not only today's Ministries of Sugar and Agriculture, but even the Ministries of Light and Heavy Industry, Transport and others.

2.2.6   The Small Farmers' Association (ANAP)

INRA was eventually phased out in 1976. But the agrarian reform had spawned a numerically and politically important sector of small private farmers, whose new organisation, the National Association of Small Farmers, ANAP (*Asociación Nacional de Agricultores Pequeños*), was to become, unlike INRA, a lasting feature of the Cuban scene and one of the most important of the revolution's 'mass organisations'.

Only small farmers, defined as those owning 5 *caballerías* (67 hectares) or less, could belong to ANAP, whose constituent assembly was held on the second anniversary of the First Agrarian Reform Law, in May 1961. By mid-1962 roughly five-sixths of them had joined.[24] The Government strongly promoted its formation for both economic and political reasons. Economically, ANAP administered the distribution of credit to small farmers, worked in coordination with INRA to encourage its members to produce crops that accorded with government priorities, and helped the authorities to purchase certain farm products at guaranteed prices. Politically, by its very existence, it drew a clear line between the self-employed small farmers (peasants) and their medium-sized counterparts (who relied on employed labour and were thus regarded as capitalists) which was to prove crucial in limiting counter-revolutionary activity when the latter were targeted for expropriation in the second phase of the reform. And in general, it provided mediation between the Government and the small farmers, and it acted as a forum for representing small farmers' concerns to the authorities.

2.2.7 The Second Agrarian Reform

The main goal of the Second Agrarian Reform was political: the expropriation of the rural capitalists, whatever their degree of efficiency, and of the few remaining landlords.[25] In the first round of expropriations, those owning between 5 and 30 *caballerías* had been left untouched, a sector that amounted to 20–25 per cent of the total land. This was the sector that was now taken over.

Again most of the land went to the state. By 1965 it is estimated that between 70 and 76 per cent of all farming land was in public ownership.[26] However, a further 40–50 000 peasants received land titles and by mid-1965 there were 199 297 peasant farmers, owning 199 554 *caballerías*, that is, an average of about 13.5 hectares per private farm. Though about half the supposed 'vital minimum' area, the quality of their holdings was generally higher than that of the state lands. It has been recorded that the 25–30 per cent of land in peasant hands represented 43 per cent of the arable land and almost 60 per cent of high quality agricultural land.[27]

At the same time, the Government issued a formal pledge that there would be no further forced expropriations. From now on farmers would be integrated into the state sector only on a strictly voluntary basis: the principle of *voluntaridad*.

This by no means implied that the superiority of state farms over private agriculture had been renounced. Any farmer who wished to sell his land to the State – whether because of old age, labour shortages or political commitment – could do so. The first of a series of plans for the indirect integration of peasant farmers was announced in 1965: the 'directed plan', aimed mainly at smaller peasants who were encouraged to link their activity to that of a neighbouring state farm. This meant they cultivated the crops indicated by the state farm in return for the appropriate credits, seeds, fertilisers, technical services and so forth, and were paid according to output delivered.

2.3 WAGE REFORM

Before the revolution income levels varied enormously, with substantial differences even for similar jobs,[28] since earnings reflected not only differentials of skill and responsibility, but also factors such as bargaining power and profitability.

Three years after the revolution, an attempt was made to rationalise the wage structure by establishing a nationwide scale fixing wage rates for the various categories of jobs. Introduced in 1962, it was fully operational by 1967, and remained in force with only minor variations until the wage and price reforms of 1981.

The new structure, involving the categorisation of workers, classification of jobs, and the establishment of wage rates and methods of payment, was a major undertaking. Large numbers of specialists had to be trained, lists of posts drawn up along with descriptions of their job content, and wage rates then had to be fixed for the different posts.[29] The scale of the task is illustrated by the fact that the number of job categories was boiled down from 10 634 to 340, and the number of grades to forty-one for the entire economy.

The major distinction that was drawn was between workers, service staff, administrative staff, technicians, and management. The category of workers was further subdivided into agricultural and non-agricultural.

Then a single salary structure was drawn up, with sixteen steps or gradations, to which were matched the various categories of workers. Agricultural workers, for example, could be classified into any one of the first seven wage brackets depending on the exact nature of their work. Management could be classified anywhere between the fifth and sixteenth steps; and technicians could receive anything between the sixth and fifteenth level of wages, depending in all cases on the exact nature of their work (see Table 2.5).

From top to bottom, the ratio between the lowest and highest wage rates was approximately 1:5.5. The minimum wage for agricultural workers was fixed at 0.33 *pesos* per hour (2.64 per day), and for non-agricultural workers at 0.43 *pesos* (3.44).

2.3.1 Work norms

A striking feature of the wage reform was its emphasis on the development of work norms, specifying output targets per hour or day for each job category. Such norms naturally lend themselves to piece rates and bonuses, but in point of fact the political tide subsequently turned strongly against 'material' in favour of 'moral incentives', and material stimuli only became generalised much later on. Thus for the time being, the payment system in industry was based firmly on hourly pay rates, with little scope for bonuses and output-linked incomes in general.

Only in agriculture were work norms employed to introduce limited piece-rate and bonus payments for labourers on the state farms,[30] until they too were abolished in the 'Revolutionary Offensive' of 1967–70.

Despite the goal of establishing a single unified wage structure, there were inevitably some anomalies. In order to pave the way for the new system, all wages had been frozen in 1961, but with the introduction of the new scale in 1962 many employees found they were earning higher salaries than those stipulated under the new provisions. Such people were allowed to retain what came to be known as their 'historic' wage. With time, however, the process of 'natural wastage' – transfers, retirements and promotions – eroded the importance of this phenomenon.

Of more enduring significance was the problem of attracting workers to jobs and sectors suffering persistent labour shortages. In general, during the 1960s the commitment to moral incentives meant that no special financial rewards were offered to encourage workers to fill such posts; they were expected to respond for the sake of society. However, there were occasions when so-called 'historic' wages were established to attract workers to a particular post, until the practice was formally done away with by the trade unions at their 1973 congress. Subsequently specific 'coefficients' were introduced to

TABLE 2.5   *Wage scales and rates prior to 1981 (pesos)*

Basic scale	Agricultural workers	Non-agricultural workers	Administrative and service workers	Technicians	Managers	Tariff		Monthly Wage*	Monthly income*
						Hourly	Daily		
I	I					0.33	2.64	62.90	
II	II					0.37	2.96	70.52	
III	III	I	I			0.43	3.44	81.96	75.00
IV	IV	II	II			0.50	4.00	95.30	86.00
V	V	III	III		I	0.58	4.64	110.55	100.00
VI	VI	IV	IV	I	II	0.67	5.36	127.70	118.00
VII	VII	V	V	II	III	0.79	6.32	150.57	138.00
VIII		VI	VI	III	IV	0.93	7.44	177.26	163.00
IX		VII	VII	IV	V	1.09	9.72	207.75	192.00
X				V	VI				211.00
XI		VIII	VIII	VI	VII	1.31	10.48	249.69	231.00
XII				VII	VIII				250.00
XIII				VIII	IX				275.00
XIV				IX	X				300.00
XV					XI				325.00
XVI					XII				350.00

* The monthly wage refers to agricultural and non-agricultural workers, while the monthly income refers to the remaining.

SOURCE   Comité Estatal de Trabajo y Seguridad Social, *Reforma general de salarios* (Havana, 1980; mimeographed) pp. 6–10.

increase basic rates in regions or industries deemed a 'socio-economic priority'.

2.3.2 The rationing system

The rationing system was introduced in March 1962,[31] at a time when shortages of food were by no means as severe as they later became. Its introduction was initially more an egalitarian measure, designed to guarantee low-income households a minimum quantity of essential food items at low cost, than a means of administering for scarcity. As the shortages grew more pronounced, however, in the mid to late 1960s, the ration book or *libreta* became a crucial policy instrument in both respects.

Even today, though many items have become available outside the rationing system, the *libreta* remains very much at the core of every-day Cuban experience, even in the rural areas – farming families are equally entitled to their quota of state-subsidised food. Therefore rationing, while a key feature of the period we are now discussing, will be described in detail in the next chapter, which outlines the main features of the Cuban economic system as it stands today.

2.4 THE RETURN TO SUGAR

The authorities appear to have assumed at the outset that agricultural diversification would complement the social and political transforma-tion they wished to implement. We have seen, for example, how former seasonal cane-cutters were taken on full-time by the new state farms in the expectation that uneven demand for their labour would be ironed out through the introduction of greater crop variety. In the event, the attempt simultaneously to transform both the social nature of production and its economic direction placed an unbearable bur-den on the country's strained finances. Around 1964 the industrialisa-tion drive slowed down and the goal of immediate diversification was abandoned.

International factors also played a vital part in this strategic shift. On the one hand, the island was experiencing extreme isolation due to the international boycott campaign against it, and on the other, the Soviet Union had agreed to new trading arrangements whereby Cuba could negotiate long-term contracts for large-scale sales of sugar at a favourable price.

The long-term aspirations were however unaltered. It was the strategy which had changed: 'diversification and industrialisation remained the goals, but it would be necessary to travel to the desired destination via the mechanisation of agriculture and the expansion of sugar production – a longer route, but a faster and safer one'.[32]

In this new context sugar came to be seen as the means whereby the island could break out of underdevelopment, rather than a symbol and cause of that underdevelopment. In 1964 and 1965 the ambitious target of a 10 million ton harvest was first hinted at, then wholeheartedly embraced. The date by which it was to be achieved was 1970.

2.4.1 All hands to the cane fields

In the drive to expand sugar production the state farm sector ran up quickly against a familiar curse; the uneven seasonal demand for labour. Now, however, the problem was less one of labour surpluses during the off season – the harvest season lengthened and the late summer and autumn could to some extent be occupied in clearing and planting new areas for sugar. Rather attention was focused on meeting the labour shortage during the peak of the harvest.

It made matters no easier that a certain local diversification had taken place. Beside the post-revolutionary flight from the rigours of cane-cutting, state farm labourers had themselves reduced their work in the canefields, preferring to cultivate their small plots of land. Access to or ownership of such plots had increased significantly since 1959, while the incentive to work on them also increased with the introduction of the rationing system from 1962 onwards.

The decision to abandon or at least postpone diversification as the solution to seasonal fluctuations in labour requirements thus paved the way for a second attempted solution; the mobilisation of paid volunteer labour on a nationwide scale during the harvest season. Once again, productivity and cost effectiveness took a back seat. The early campaigns drew heavily on volunteers with little or no experience of cutting cane, who came from urban areas and worked for relatively short periods of time. Throughout the economy work was liable to disruption as volunteers responded to the needs of the sugar harvest, reaching a climax in the '10 million ton' harvest of 1970 when the rest of the economy came to a virtual standstill in the attempt to meet what proved in any case to be an overambitious target.

With voluntary work the authorities hoped to transfer, albeit temporarily, some of the surplus urban labour back to the country-side. But politically and ideologically the mobilisation campaigns were far more than this, becoming a feature of the revolutionary tradition which remains strong today, as well as pointing the cities' attentions once again towards the rural zones.

In terms of sheer numbers they were extremely successful; from 106 000 in 1966 as many as 700 000 were mobilised for 1970.[33] But the costs were high, both in terms of transport and forfeited production. Not all the labour was surplus, and since workhands were also recruited from the private farming sector's mutual aid brigades it is likely that even food output suffered.

Undoubtedly a far more effective answer to the labour shortages in Cuban agriculture during the 1960s would have been mechanisation. As far as sugar is concerned, however, only the loading of cane on to the mill transport was significantly mechanised during this period, with grab lifters (*alzadoras*) doing more than 80 per cent of this work by 1970,[34] compared with the 1964 figure of 20 per cent.

The task of mechanising the harvest itself through the development of combine harvesters, was a far more daunting project, and took many years of research and development. By 1970 only 1 per cent of the crop was harvested mechanically. The major breakthrough in the mechanisation of cane-cutting took place only in the second half of the 1970s.

2.5 POLICY DEBATE

2.5.1 'Material' or 'moral' incentives?

In the mid-1960s, as the authorities came to grips with the problems involved in developing the country with a renewed emphasis on sugar production, an important debate developed on how to organise the economy, which touched on everything from the management of enterprises and the role of work incentives to the nature of the transition to socialism and communism.[35] This is not the place to discuss the full ramifications of this complex debate, but it is relevant to note that arguments in favour of a highly centralised 'budgetary financing system' were pitted against those for decentralisation, incentives and 'self-financing'. These contrasting themes have re-peatedly surfaced ever since.

The first formulation implied that the State should take the entire financial responsibility for the performance of state enterprises, providing non-repayable grants through the state budget, and soaking up either profits or losses as they ensued. Its advocates argued that production should be for need and not profit, that it would enable surplus to be redirected towards the less well-off regions and enterprises, and that it was in any case necessary for the country to concentrate its scarce managerial and technical skills.

The 'self-financers' stressed instead the importance of flexibility. They said credits should be repaid at appropriate rates of interest, and the autonomy of state enterprises should include financial responsibility for profits and losses, with profits used for reinvestment by the enterprise itself. In such a set-up material incentives would play an important role, being closely linked to labour productivity, in order to stimulate maximum efficiency.

2.5.2   The 'Revolutionary Offensive'

It was increasingly the 'budgetary financing' criteria that prevailed. The centralisation reached its climax with the proclamation of the 'Revolutionary Offensive' in 1968. Its main feature was the expropriation of all remaining private business, except the small private farmers.[36]

Monetary calculations were downgraded, and in the context of transactions within the state sector itself, abandoned altogether. Interest charges of all kinds were eliminated, and many taxes. Enterprises gave minimal priority to cost accounting and were encouraged to do so. Piece rates and bonuses of all kinds were abandoned as absolute pride of place was given to 'moral incentives'.[37] Even time rates were supplanted for a period by the introduction in many industrial workplaces of 'conscience time' – *horario de conciencia* – whereby attendance was deemed a matter for the workers' own revolutionary consciousness. Wage differentials were further reduced in the drive for egalitarianism. It was a conscious and, as it turned out, a damaging and premature attempt to introduce the communist maxim: 'From each according to ability, to each according to need.'

However, there were not only ideological objections to a comprehensive system of material incentives. We have seen how initially the unified wage system of 1962 could have lent itself to piece rates and bonuses on the basis of the work norms that were defined for each job category. But to function efficiently the work norms had to be accurate, and they were still in the process of formation and definition. If norms were high workers would complain, whereas if they were low they would relax. There was a still more fundamental limitation. Extensive shortages and strict rationing now meant that the problem for workers was less that of earning money than spending it. It was hard to convert extra cash into extra consumption.[38] Free social services helped reduce the urgency for workers to maximise earnings, and the shortages undermined it even more.

On the state farms, the only sector where piece rates and bonuses had been made operative, they were now abandoned. A campaign was launched to restrict access to small plots – a source of considerable frustration that has only recently been tackled with the introduction of collective 'self-provision' systems (*autoconsumo*). Black market activity surged as farm prices were lowered.[39]

2.5.3   Integration of private farmers

With private economic activity of all kinds under ideological siege, the small farming sector attracted close attention as the Government, while still formally committed to the principle of *voluntaridad*, made special efforts to integrate the peasant owners into the state farm sector.

The Government's standing offer to buy out farmers whose old age, labour shortages or political commitment made them willing to sell was not taken up on any great scale.[40] During the Revolutionary Offensive, however, the pace of change quickened and by the early 1970s as many as 30 000 had been purchased,[41] representing some 16 per cent of private land. Whereas during the agrarian reform the state had absorbed mostly the poorer land under extensive cultivation, its acquisitions during this period were of higher quality, and accounted for 25 per cent of arable land previously in private hands.[42]

Some of the purchases, despite the principle of *voluntaridad*, were made compulsorily, primarily around the major cities like Havana where the State had created 'green belt' zones in which it was making special investments. These areas were also a significant source of the black market produce.[43]

Other forms of integration which were strongly promoted during the late 1960s can be described as indirect, since while they involved farmers linking themselves to the production plan of a nearby state farm, they were not expected to give up their land titles. Like the 'directed plan' launched in 1964–5, the 'specialised plan' implemented in 1967 gave peasants the inputs they needed to fulfil their quotas, which were determined by the state farm. Farmers were paid according to output. Just over half of all private farmers joined either 'directed' or 'specialised' plans during the Revolutionary Offensive, although their holdings amounted to only about one-sixth of private lands.[44]

The 'integral plan', also launched in 1967, attracted only about 2 in 15 private farmers, although their holdings tended to be larger, since they represented a further one-sixth of all private lands. The scheme involved leasing to the State in return for an annual rent. The farmer might retain the house and a small plot but he and his family were encouraged to work as labourers for the state farm.

The largest of the small farmers, however, tended to remain aloof from such plans altogether. A third of the total declined to join, but they held two-thirds of the private lands.

2.6 THE FIRST DECADE ASSESSED

In terms of the Government's social and political goals, the hectic process of agrarian reform after the 1959 revolution must be counted a success. Well before 1970 foreign agribusiness, the landlord class and the medium capitalist farmers had all disappeared from the scene. The seasonal labourers enjoyed guaranteed full-time employment on the new state farms. By 1965, the number of full-time privately hired wage workers in agriculture had been reduced to a mere 36 000,[45] and by 1970 the figure had fallen to 24 100.

Unemployment itself had fallen from 11.8 per cent in 1960 to 1.3 per cent in 1970. The state had taken effective control of the land, exercising direct administration of more than 70 per cent and enjoying through the peasants' organisation, ANAP, majority support of those who worked the remainder. Militarily, also, counter-revolution in the countryside had been stifled. And the rural population, for all the consumer shortages, was witnessing clear benefits from the Government's programmes for education, health and other social priorities.

The decade also saw many economic improvements that were to provide an important basis for expansion and development in the future. The thousands of small water reservoirs that today dot the Cuban landscape are perhaps the most visible feature of the rural investments made during those years, enabling the area of land under irrigation to increase by 73 per cent between 1960 and 1970. Roads, transport, machinery and equipment – as well as education and health – had all been the target of major investments.

2.6.1   Employment promotion

Former seasonal workers were given full-time employment on the state farms from 1962 without regard to their productivity during the slack season. It was accepted that the workload was insufficient to absorb all of them productively, but since the overall economic strategy was one of agricultural diversification it was initially anticipated that labour requirements during the traditional off-season would expand, sooner rather than later, to absorb all these workers productively.

The pool of unemployed farmworkers had in any case diminished; some had responded to the opportunities opening up in the towns – many of the cane-cutters had traditionally been drawn from urban areas. Others had found employment in the expanding sector of social services in rural areas. Farmers, with their own plots now validated by title-deeds, reverted to full-time private farming. The sheer hardship of cane-cutting itself, an arduous and back-breaking job, was good enough reason to take advantage of such openings. This actually meant, curiously enough, that the pronounced 'proletarianisation' tendencies of the 1950s had not only been halted but actually reversed, if only temporarily, by a revolution now openly proclaiming the leading role of the industrial working class.

The consequence, especially once the emphasis on sugar was renewed around 1964, was both a sharp reduction of the surplus of rural labour during the slack season and an even more pronounced deficit of labour during the harvest, requiring the mobilisation of up to 700 000 cane-cutters. Mechanisation of the sugar harvest was one answer, but the development of a specialised combine harvester capable of dealing with a crop the size of sugar cane still lay in the future. The most immediate way the fieldworkers' – and the labour planners' – burden could be relieved in the short term was through the introduction of grab-lifters to load the cut cane on to the mill transport.

2.6.2   Redistribution of income

Immediately after the revolution there was a massive redistribution of income from the rich to the poor, under the impact of such policies as the expropriation of the estates and plantations, the abolition of land rent and the imposition of stiff housing rent controls in the urban areas, a sharp increase in employment, and an increase in the real wage of around 20 per cent.[46]

It is hard to put precise figures on this trend, but its overall direction is quite clear. As far as the bottom 40 per cent are concerned, their share of all household income shot up by something in the order of 50 per cent between 1958 and 1962, from 14.6 per cent of the national total to 21.7 per cent.[47] The fact that a single uniform scale, narrowing down the ratio between lowest and highest wages to 1:5.5 could be introduced in 1962 (and fully operative by 1967) is itself indicative of the impact of egalitarian policies.

While some non-wage earners, such as the richer small farmers, have continued to earn more than the top salary to this day, the progressive state takeover of private enterprises also meant that household incomes came to rely more and more heavily on wages, making the equalisation of wage levels even more significant. The first wave of nationalisations left only some 20 per cent of the economy in private hands by the end of 1961,[48] and the nationalisation of the remainder of the private sector in 1968 left primarily the private farms. Such measures not only had the effect of boosting lower incomes, but brought incomes at the top end of the scale down with a considerable bump. By 1962, the top 20 per cent found their collective household income had fallen to 46.5 per cent from 54.6 per cent of the national total in 1958. This was in part the result of wealthy Cubans leaving the country – some 215 000 individuals left during this period.[49]

Meanwhile, the rapid expansion of social provisions such as free health and education services also had a strong equalising effect on real living standards, increasing the relative weight of the 'social wage' and reducing the significance of such income differentials – themselves diminished – as persisted. The same can be said of the progressive introduction of the rationing system. Indeed, amid growing shortages of consumer goods, personal income came to bear only a restricted relation to consumption itself. With money in their pockets, individuals and households found their intake determined as much by availability as purchasing power.

Interestingly, while the poorest 40 per cent appear to have been the leading beneficiaries of the very early years, it is the middle band that appears to have increased its share of income most in the decade after 1962. Between 1962 and 1973 personal income of the bottom 40 per cent increased from 17.2 per cent of the total to 18.3 per cent.

The 20 per cent above saw their share rise from 16.3 to 19.2 per cent.[50] The overall trend nevertheless continued; the programme of nationalisations, culminating in the state takeover of small businesses in 1968, adversely affected many of those whose earnings from profits had been significantly above national levels.[51] Even in the farming sector, only 25–30 per cent of the land remained in private hands by the early 1970s.[52] The proportion of personal income enjoyed by the top 20 per cent fell from 41.4 per cent in 1962 to 34.5 per cent in 1973.

These results suggest that the very poor benefited most from the land expropriation and redistribution programme, rent controls and other measures enacted after 1959. They benefited less from the introduction of the uniform wage scale or, in the later 1960s, the elimination of many bonus and overtime payments as part of the overall emphasis on moral (as opposed to material) incentives.

2.6.3 Economic performance

As far as output and efficiency are concerned, the agrarian sector had fared less well. Overall output in terms of the conventional measure of gross domestic product averaged a meagre 1.5 per cent annual growth between 1961 and 1970, with agriculture growing at the same rate, in both cases failing to keep pace with the rapid population growth of around 2.3 per cent. The state farms had increased their share of this declining per capita farm production from 57.7 per cent in 1964 to 65 per cent in 1968 and 71.1 per cent in 1970 – roughly in line with the increase in their total area.[53] But this probably reflects more on the disruption of the private sector – and possibly the growth of the black market – than on their own achievements.

The poor performance is not hard to explain. There were major institutional changes as more than 80 per cent of the economy was transferred to state control; there was the imposition of an economic boycott, observed by almost all of the western hemisphere, which enforced a complete reorientation of trade and capital flows; there was a massive outflow of skilled professionals and technicians; a substantial increase in defence spending; a comprehensive shake-up of development priorities, economic planning and management methods; and towards the end of the decade, the virtual abolition of internal accounting methods and material incentives. In the light of all these factors it is perhaps surprising that per capita output did not fall more significantly during the period.

But as the 1970s started, with the leadership in self-critical mood, no one was suggesting that explanations alone might address the problems. It was time for another change of direction.

NOTES AND REFERENCES

1. A. MacEwan, *Revolution and economic development in Cuba* (London: Macmillan, 1981) p. 3.
2. J. Acosta, 'La estructura agraria y el sector agropecuario al triunfo de la revolución', in *Economía y Desarrollo*, 1972, no. 9, p. 57.
3. M. Gutelman, *La agricultura socializada en Cuba* (Mexico: Ediciones Era, 1970) p. 17.
4. B. H. Pollitt, *Agrarian reform and the 'agricultural proletariat' in Cuba, 1958–66: Some notes* (Institute of Latin American Studies Occasional Papers, University of Glasgow, 1979) no. 27, pp. 4, 5 and table 6.
5. Data from the *Consejo Nacional de Economía* quoted in C. Mesa-Lago, 'The labour force, employment, unemployment and underemployment in Cuba: 1899–1970' (Beverly Hills: Sage Publications, 1972) p. 22.
6. Ibid., p. 24.
7. J. Chonchol, 'El primer bienio de reforma agraria (1959–1961)', in O. Delgado (ed.) *Reformas agrarias en América Latina* (Mexico: Fondo de Cultura Económica, 1965) pp. 470–1.
8. A. Bianchi, 'Agriculture: The pre-revolutionary background', in D. Seers (ed.), *Cuba, the economic and social revolution* (Chapel Hill: The University of North Carolina Press, 1964) p. 79.
9. J. Martínez-Alier, *Haciendas, plantations and collective farms: Agrarian class societies – Cuba and Peru* (London: Frank Cass, 1977) pp. 100–1.
10. J. I. Domínguez, *Cuba: Order and revolution* (Cambridge, Mass: Harvard University Press, 1978) p. 421.
11. A. Bianchi, op. cit., pp. 72–3 and J. Acosta, op. cit., pp. 80–1.
12. C. R. Rodríguez, *Letra con filo* (Havana: Editorial de Ciencias Sociales, 1983) vol. 2, p. 248.
13. J. Acosta, 'Las leyes de reforma agraria en Cuba y el sector privado campesino', in *Economía y Desarrollo*, no. 12, 1972, p. 99.
14. Different figures are given by C. R. Rodríguez, op. cit., p. 240; A. MacEwan, op. cit., p. 56; and N. Forster, 'The revolutionary transformation of the Cuban countryside', in *UFSI Reports* (Universities Field Staff International, 1982) no. 26, p. 2.
15. A. MacEwan, op. cit., p. 56.
16. Ibid., p. 57.
17. See also O. Trinchet, *La cooperativización de la tierra en el agro cubano* (Havana: Editora Política, 1984) p. 24.
18. J. Chonchol, op. cit., p. 490.
19. Ibid., p. 491.
20. Ibid., p. 495.
21. J. I. Domínguez, op. cit., p. 449; and V. Bondarchuk, 'Formas y métodos de incorporación de los agricultores a la economía socialista de Cuba', *América Latina*, no. 4 (20), 1978, pp. 18–19.

22. J. Acosta, 'La revolución agraria en Cuba y el desarrollo económico', *Revista Interamericana de Planificación*, vol. 8, no. 28–29 (Bogotá) December 1973–March 1974, p. 55.
23. F. Castro, *Informe del Comité Central del Partido Comunista de Cuba al Primer Congreso* (Havana: Editorial de Ciencias Sociales, 1978).
24. J. Chonchol, 'Análisis crítico de la reforma agraria cubana', in *El Trimestre Económico*, vol. 30, no. 117, 1963, p. 130; and A. Martin Barrios, *La ANAP: 20 Años de Trabajo* (Havana: n.p., 1982) p. 26.
25. C. R. Rodríguez, 'La segunda reforma agraria cubana: causas y derivaciones', in O. Delgado (ed.), *Reformas agrarias en América Latina* (Mexico: Fondo de Cultura Económica, 1965) p. 527.
26. Among the authors who give a 70 per cent estimate are C. R. Rodríguez, 'The Cuban revolution and the peasantry', in *World Marxist Review*, vol. 8, no. 10, 1965, p. 19; P. Gey, 'Die Kollektivierung der kleinbäuerlichen Landwirtschaft in Kuba', in *Agrarwirtschaft*, vol. 33, no. 7, 1984, p. 210; and V. Bondarchuk, op. cit., p. 21. A 71 per cent figure is given by Trinchet, op. cit., p. 24, and a 76 per cent by J. Acosta, 'Las leyes . . .', op. cit., p. 108, and A. MacEwan, op. cit., p. 73. A lower figure of 60 per cent, which in our view is an underestimate, is given by M. Gutelman, op. cit., p. 62.
27. V. Bondarchuk, op. cit., p. 21 and J. I. Domínguez, op. cit., p. 455. According to A. MacEwan, op. cit., p. 197, and M. Benjamin, J. Collins and M. Scott, *No free lunch: Food and revolution in Cuba today* (San Francisco: Institute for Food and Development Policy, 1984) p. 162, the private sector held 37 per cent of the cultivated land and according to J. Acosta, 'Las leyes . . .', p. 108, also the same percentage of the cultivable land.
28. José Acosta, *Teoría y práctica de los mecanismos de dirección de la economía en Cuba* (Havana: Editorial de Ciencias Sociales, 1982).
29. For more details, see I. Talavera and J. R. Herrera, 'La organización del trabajo y el salario en la agricultura', in *Cuba Socialista*, vol. 5, no. 45/46 (Havana), May–June 1965.
30. Ibid., pp. 56–79.
31. M. Benjamin, J. Collins and M. Scott, op. cit., p. 23.
32. J. C. Edelstein, 'The evolution of Cuban development strategy, 1959–1980', in H. Muñoz (ed.), *From dependency to development: Strategies to overcome underdevelopment and inequality* (Boulder, Col: Westview Press, 1982) p. 234.
33. C. Mesa-Lago, *The economy of socialist Cuba: A two-decade appraisal* (Albuquerque: University of New Mexico Press, 1981) p. 129.
34. República de Cuba, Comité Estatal de Estadísticas, *Cuba: desarrollo económico y social durante el período 1958–1980* (Havana, 1981) p. 67, and C. Edquist, 'Mechanisation of sugar cane harvesting', in *Cuban Studies*, vol. 13, no. 2, 1983, p. 47.
35. See B. Silverman (ed.), *Man and socialism in Cuba – The great debate* (New York: Atheneum, 1971); J. Martínez-Alier, op. cit., ch. 6; and N. P. Valdés, 'The Cuban revolution: Economic organisation and

bureaucracy', in *Latin American Perspectives*, vol. 6, no. 1, issue 20, 1979, pp. 13–37.
36. There were some other minor exceptions: the ancient and battered vehicles of a few private self-employed truck and taxi owners can still be seen rattling along the streets of Havana, while a couple of hundred private doctors, qualified before 1959, who neither joined the state system nor fled the country, have retained their practices to this day.
37. A. R. M. Ritter, *The economic development of revolutionary Cuba: Strategy and performance* (New York: Praeger, 1974) pp. 269–82.
38. R. M. Bernardo, 'Moral stimulation as a non-market mode of labour allocation in Cuba', in *Studies in Comparative International Development*, vol. 6, no. 6, 1970–1, p. 127.
39. N. Forster, op. cit., pp. 6–7.
40. J. I. Domínguez, op. cit., p. 453.
41. O. Trinchet, op. cit., p. 28.
42. Ibid., pp. 23, 28, 29, and J. I. Domínguez, op. cit., p. 455.
43. D. F. Otero, 'Agricultura y planeamiento. El caso de Cuba', in *Desarrollo y Sociedad*, vol. 1, no. 1, 1979, p. 155, and P. Peek, *Collectivising the peasantry: The Cuban experience*, Draft Paper (Geneva: ILO, 1984) p. 27.
44. C. Auroi, *La nouvelle agriculture cubaine* (Paris: Editions Anthropos, 1975) p. 54, and J. Acosta, 'La revolución . . .', op. cit., p. 57.
45. S. Aranda, *La revolución agraria en Cuba* (Mexico D.F.: Siglo XXI Editores, 1969) p. 148.
46. R. Dumont, *Cuba: Socialisme et développement* (Paris: Editions du Seuil, 1964) p. 43.
47. A. MacEwan, op. cit., p. 229.
48. Ibid.
49. C. Mesa-Lago, 1972, op. cit., p. 41.
50. C. Brundenius, *Revolutionary Cuba: The challenges of economic growth with equity* (Boulder: Westview Press, 1986) pp. 114–16.
51. A. MacEwan, op. cit., p. 229.
52. P. Peek, *From peasant to collective farmer: Cuba's third agrarian reform* (Geneva: ILO, 1986; mimeographed).
53. S. Aranda, op. cit., p. 36; República de Cuba, Comité Estatal de Estadísticas, 1981, op. cit., p. 61; and Comité Estatal de Estadísticas, *Annario Estadístico de Cuba 1983* (Havana, 1984) p. 191.

3 The Economy and Agriculture

The policies of the late 1960s dislocated the economy in many regions of the countryside, and indeed throughout the country as a whole. Absenteeism had reached the point where one worker in five was away from work at any one time as there was so little material urgency to attend. The huge mobilisations of voluntary labour, culminating in 1970 when 700 000 took part in the *zafra*, did not achieve the desired results, while severely disrupting the rest of the economy. Farm production was stagnant, and relations between the State and the private farming sector had been badly strained by the Revolutionary Offensive.

The mistakes were in some respects an echo of the early years, an attempt to make the economy run before it could walk. On the first occasion, it had been a bid to diversify production at the same time as transforming its ownership, management structures and labour processes, whereas reality showed that diversification was a longer term task for which the foundations had to be created first. This time it had been a bid to leapfrog socialism itself: the explicit attempt to head directly towards communist principles of production.

There ensued a major shift in overall economic policy that marks out the year 1970 as a critical watershed. It was not until the mid-1970s that really major initiatives emerged, but this itself may reflect a new determination to proceed with caution. Certainly, from the beginning of the decade onwards, work norms and the financial accountability of enterprises were reintroduced as the taboos against material incentives, profit-and-loss accounting, and other features of a 'self-financing' approach were consciously broken down.

The First Congress of the Cuban Communist Party (PCC) in 1975 gave full expression to such attitudes. Initiatives to 'institutionalise' the island's political, legal and social life swiftly followed, including a new constitution and the People's Power system of elected municipal, provincial and national government, to list only the most significant.

Meanwhile, on the economic front the First Congress of the PCC heralded the creation of a comprehensive system of planning, the Economic Management and Planning System, or SDPE (*Sistema de Dirección Planificación Económica*), unambiguously proclaiming the principles of 'self-financing' which had received such short shrift only a decade earlier.[1] The Congress also consolidated a shift in development strategy towards agricultural machinery and industrial investment and away from farming.[2]

The Second Congress of the PCC, in December 1980, took these principles a stage further, declaring 'the *peso* should really control all economic activity'[3] and clarifying the other main features of the emerging planning system.

The Third Congress, in February 1986, was a further landmark. Once again there was a detailed examination of the planning system, including severe criticism of weaknesses, and particularly the application of unrealistic prices which 'only serve to cover up inefficiency' that, if not overcome, would mean that the central planning system 'would cease to be the driving force of the economy'.[4] The main guidelines for resolving these problems and promoting economic efficiency were established.

This chapter sets out to describe the main aspects of Cuba's economic system as it stands today, and particularly as it affects the farming sector and rural development. It takes as its starting point the most prominent features of the SDPE as they were formulated by the Second Congress of the PCC.

3.1   THE NEW MANAGEMENT PRINCIPLES

Comprehensive planning

> All enterprises should be included in the system of economic accounting.

Decentralisation

> The operational economic autonomy of the enterprises should be fully observed . . . The director of each enterprise would be given enough real authority . . . Patronage and guardianship by the central agencies and local administrations should be avoided.[5]

Internal accounting

On the same occasion, the Communist Party called for a higher degree of economic efficiency and output, to achieve which it announced plans for a shake-up of the price system and urged:

> Constant efforts will be made . . . to organise or introduce and consolidate, work norms; norms for material required for each product and service; technical norms for use of machinery, equipment and facilities; inventory quotas; norms for quality specifications; and financial norms.[6]

Material incentives

Parallel to the price reform there was to be a wage reform and:

> the principle of payment (should be) determined by the quantity and quality of work . . . and the development of quotas . . . The 'flexible' portion of wages should be increased by means of bonuses that stimulate the fulfilment of economic efficiency . . . This flexible portion should constitute at least 15 to 25 per cent of the worker's total wage . . . (And) direct contracting of the work force should be extended.[7]

3.1.1 A comprehensive planning system

Each year the State Planning Board JUCEPLAN (*Junta Central de Planificación*) prepares its national economic plan, in consultation with the Party. In the first, provisional stage, it is known as the Control Plan (*Plan de Control*) and contains output targets or 'control figures' (*cifras de control*), derived from a complex set of calculations based on existing data. These goals cover the economy as a whole, each sector of the economy – such as agriculture – and each branch of activity within each sector.

In general, the Control Plan also assigns the relevant inputs, both capital and labour, that it considers necessary to achieve these goals, which means that not only are targets set for production, but also, and equally explicitly, for productivity as well. On the peasant cooperatives and individual farms, however, since labour levels are not directly dictated by the state, only their output targets are covered by the *cifras de control*.

The 'control figures' are then discussed within the ministries. In agriculture, for example, the Sugar and Agriculture Ministries disaggregate them and work out their meaning for each region, sector, state farm or union of state farms, collective or union of collectives, private farmers' credit and service cooperatives, and so on.

Only when these targets reach the lower levels does the second planning stage begin as the producers themselves examine the implications. The specifics of this negotiation process vary, of course, between the state farms, the collectives (CPAs) and the individual private farmers, and each will be described in its appropriate place. But in one way or another, the producers respond to the *cifra de control* with their own proposal as to what the final 'directive' or 'mandatory' figure should be; their *propuesta de cifra directiva*.

This proposal then travels back up the administrative ladder and finally, in the third stage, a Directive Plan (*Plan Directivo*) is adopted, comprising contractually binding 'directive figures' (*cifras directivas*) for each unit of the economy.

3.1.2 Restructuring the farm sector

The Agrarian Reform Institute (INRA) survived until 1976, long after the agrarian reform itself was complete. So widespread were the responsibilities it acquired in the early years that it had already spawned a Ministry of Industry, and on its demise INRA's remaining duties fell to a new Ministry of Agriculture, or MINAG (*Ministerio de Agricultura*). Meanwhile, the industrial sector was distributed between the Ministries of Light Industry (MINIL), Basic Industry (MINBAS) and the Sugar Industry, the latter with responsibilities for the sugar mills.

In 1980, it was decided to integrate sugar cultivation and the mills under one administrative roof by creating Agro-industrial Complexes, or CAIs (*Complejos Agro-Industriales*). It was hoped that this could improve coordination between the agricultural and industrial spheres, and give the mills greater authority to insist on punctual deliveries, less impurities in the cane and higher quality in general. The CAIs, which became the responsibility of a renamed Ministry of Sugar or MINAZ (*Ministerio de Azúcar*), developed rapidly. From four in 1981, there are now 143 of them, accounting for virtually all the sugar cane state farms.[8] The farming sector is thus now the joint domain of MINAG and MINAZ. Both have their central offices in Havana and provincial offices in each of the fourteen provinces.

In 1986, the Third Congress of the PCC formalised the role of a 'central group' of the Council of State, set up in late 1984, with trouble-shooting powers to intervene wherever major bottle-necks might threaten the smooth functioning of the economy, and foresaw the creation of a new 'superministry' to oversee the planning process.[9]

3.1.3 Decentralisation

The aims of the most recent innovations, whose practical effects remain to be seen, include a far greater measure of autonomy and flexibility. Already, compared to the situation before the introduction of the SDPE, the planning system has brought considerably greater scope for enterprises to influence the size of their production targets. There is no clear indication, however, from the documents of the Third Congress, that local autonomy will include the scope to embark, for example, on independent investment initiatives funded out of profits.[10]

Explicitly ruling out any significant role for the market mechanism, the Cuban authorities thus appear to see autonomy in terms of localised control over the practical task of fulfilling the agreed targets.

3.1.4 Labour policy

This obviously means that labour, like other inputs, must be deliberately assigned to enterprises as part of the plan, and indeed a complex structure has evolved to enable this to happen. Within the Control Plan labour requirements are estimated by economic sector and by region, taking into account production targets, productivity levels, investments and so forth, and an estimate is made similarly of the availability of labour within each sector and region. Numbers of school leavers, retirements and military service are all factors that have to be taken into account.

The State Committee on Labour (*Comité Estatal de Trabajo*) provides a set of criteria or guidelines, and in particular specifies what it sees as an appropriate ratio of administrative and service workers to directly 'productive' employees within any particular sector or type of enterprise.

The enterprises themselves, meanwhile, as part of the planning process, may well lobby for adjustments to be made to their *plantilla* or labour force. (The term *plantilla* refers not merely to the sheer numbers of workers, but also the workforce's composition in terms of skills, qualifications and job descriptions.) Between the enterprise, the *Comité Estatal de Trabajo* and the appropriate ministry, like other aspects of the plan, an agreement is finally arrived at which is legally binding on the parties concerned.

Once the labour has been assigned, however, it may need to be recruited. And similarly a worker seeking employment needs a channel through which to find work. This is largely the responsibility of the People's Power (*Poder Popular*, the Cuban system of national and municipal government). The present book does not attempt to provide a comprehensive discussion of the People's Power system, whose novel features have attracted the attention of many analysts and commentators. As far as administrating the supply of labour is concerned, each municipality has a labour office or *Dirección de Trabajo* which, in close consultation with the *Comité Estatal de Trabajo* prepares a local balance-sheet or *Balance Laboral* specifying the number and type of workers required in the region, and those available. If it is not possible to match the first to the second, then it may be possible to resolve the problem by contacting a neighbouring municipality.

Before 1980, it was obligatory for all workers seeking jobs – and particularly those leaving school to enter the job 'market' – to contact the local labour office. However, as labour shortages began to ease individuals were permitted to make direct contact with enterprises.[11] Even when a worker is taken on directly by the enterprise without using the 'clearing-house' functions of the People's Power system – and in general workers prefer to organise their own employment if possible to avoid being assigned a job they consider inappropriate or undesirable – the relevant authorities must be advised of the fact, and the appointment must comply with the enterprise's agreed *plantilla*.

Volunteer labour and student labour are also included in the *Balance Laboral* drawn up by the local People's Power authorities, and it is their task to ensure that sectors heavily reliant on voluntary mobilisations (notably construction and sugar harvesting) or school labour (above all citrus cultivation) have a properly coordinated labour supply.

The issue of workers' dismissals represents a further important responsibility of the labour authorities, although as well as the *Comité Estatal de Trabajo* and the People's Power labour office, the trade unions and the legal tribunals are inevitably drawn in whenever dismissals occur.

Dismissals in a country which proclaims workers' power are inevitably a vexed question. For many years it was legally virtually impossible for any worker to be sacked, and even since the introduction of the SDPE in the mid-1970s, only limited powers of dismissal have been available to enterprise administration. In general, it can be stated that workers are only ever removed from their jobs on the basis of misconduct – rather than, for example, economic superfluity.

In controlling, limiting and, where relevant, reducing the size of an enterprise's workforce it is therefore the recruitment of new labour to take the place of retirements that is the principal instrument. The more recent emphasis on matching the size of an enterprise's workforce to economic requirements is accordingly reflected in the fact that in 1981, when open unemployment totalled only 3.4 per cent of the workforce, the percentage of unemployed among 17 to 19-year-olds was 17.1 per cent.[12] This reflects the waiting period – sometimes three to four months – that a number of school graduates face before their first job.

3.2   WAGES AND INCENTIVES

The national wage scale introduced in 1962 remained in force for almost two decades virtually unaltered. The changes in average levels of take-home pay during this time were the result either of changes in the structure of the workforce or of fluctuations in the official policy on material incentives – which affected the 'flexible' portion of workers' incomes. Without specific legislation, the reintroduction of piece rates and bonuses during the course of the 1970s meant that nearly 719 000 workers or 36 per cent of the total working in production were on piece rate systems by September 1979, and 600 000 workers regularly received bonuses for meeting and/or overfulfilling their work norms.[13]

3.2.1   The 1981 wage reform

The wage reform of 1981 had several aims. It sought to streamline and modernise the wage system by bringing job classifications, wage rates and scales into line with the changing skills of the labour force and the growing complexities of the economy. It attempted to make wages fairer by removing outstanding anomalies. And it sought actively to promote bonuses and piece rates in line with the new emphasis on incentives in national economic planning and management methods.

The new salary scale is shown in Table 3.1 (the earlier salary scale was given in Table 2.5). Its main features were:

(1) A general increase in minimum wage rates, for each category, with proportionately larger increases for workers in the lower categories;
(2) A comprehensive recategorisation, particularly of technical and managerial grades;
(3) An increased basic salary differential between the top and the bottom within these categories.

However, the basic salary differential between the lowest paid agricultural worker and the highest paid manager, or technician, remained fixed at approximately 1:5.5.

The minimum wage for the lowest paid workers in agriculture rose by 30 per cent, and in non-agriculture by 14 per cent. In administration and services, minimum wages increased about 13 per cent, while the bottom salaries for technical and managerial personnel increased 8 per cent and 11 per cent, respectively.

In relative terms, the higher the worker within the lower categories, the smaller was the increase. For instance, while basic rates for non-agricultural workers on step 1 were 14 per cent more after the reform, the basic rates for step 7 were only 3.4 per cent greater. For administration and services workers these percentages were 13 for step 1 and 0 for step 9. In the case of technicians and managers, the higher steps showed larger relative increases.

In the second feature of the reform was the addition of more 'rungs' at the top of the salary 'ladder', so that overall there were now twenty-two grades instead of sixteen. But different jobs were affected differently.

For farm labourers the number of grades decreased from seven to four; this is because skilled agricultural workers were amalgamated into the category of non-agricultural workers, which, as before, had eight grades. The number of grades for administrative and service staff also remained unchanged, at eight.

For technical staff, by contrast, there were now nineteen grades instead of ten, and for management, twenty instead of twelve. This was in order to improve incentives for these categories – managers and technicians in general do not qualify for performance bonuses except, as shown further on, in the permanent production brigades (BPPs). As a result, basic rates for the top categories of the new wage

TABLE 3.1   *Wage scales and rates since 1981 (pesos)*

Basic scale	Agricultural workers		Non-agricultural workers		Administrative and service workers	Technicians			Recently graduated			Managers
	Hourly rate	Monthly wage	Hourly rate	Monthly wage	Monthly income	I	II	III	Low	Medium	High	Monthly income
I	0.43	81.96	0.49	93.39	85							
II	0.50	95.30	0.56	106.74	97							
III	0.58	110.55	0.64	121.98	111				111.00			111.00
IV	0.67	127.70	0.74	141.04	128	128.00	138.00	148.00				128.00
V			0.85	162.01	148	148.00	160.00	171.00		148.00		148.00
VI			0.98	186.79	171	171.00	185.00	198.00				171.00
VII			1.14	217.28	198	198.00	205.00	211.00			198.00	198.00
VIII						211.00	221.00	231.00				211.00
IX			1.33	254.02	231	231.00	250.00	265.00				231.00
X						250.00	265.00	280.00				250.00
XI						265.00	280.00	295.00				265.00
XII						280.00	295.00	310.00				280.00
XIII						295.00	310.00	325.00				295.00
XIV						310.00	325.00	340.00				310.00
XV						325.00	340.00	355.00				325.00
XVI						340.00						340.00
XVII						355.00						355.00
XVIII						370.00						370.00
XIX						385.00						385.00
XX						400.00						400.00
XXI						425.00						425.00
XXII						450.00						450.00

SOURCE   Unpublished documentation from Comité Estatal de Trabajo y Seguridad Social.

scale actually increased very considerably – by 29 per cent and 38 per cent for managers and technicians respectively – and the ratio between basic earnings in their lowest and highest grades increased.

For technical staff a further refinement was introduced. Within each grade, the revised salary structure introduced three incremental steps. Given a satisfactory performance, staff in such posts can move up a step every year. But they can only be promoted into a new grade by qualifying to fill a vacancy at that level. All such promotions are dependent on having the required qualifications and experience.

3.2.2 Job premiums

The introduction of the unified salary structure in 1962, followed by the smothering of piece rates and bonuses in the late 1960s, effectively reduced productivity linked wages for a time from the Cuban economy. But instruments did survive whereby workers could be paid extra to work in hazardous, strategic or hard-to-fill posts; the special premiums or 'coefficients' for industries, regions and occupations of particular 'economic and social interest' (*coeficientes de interés económico-social*).

Amid today's greater emphasis on material incentives, these job premiums have been employed on a greater scale. As far as this book is concerned, the most important example is the sugar sector where all workers from labourers to managers earn 15 per cent over the basic rate. But workers in nickel, construction, mining and quarrying also enjoy significant premiums.

Seniority also entitles workers to higher pay in certain occupations, with the sugar industry again the most important example – all workers earn an extra 5 per cent after five years' service, with an additional increment after ten years. Similar benefits operate for school teachers and some building workers.

Finally night-workers and others on special shifts also receive a premium of 8 *centavos* an hour or about 15 *pesos* a month.

3.2.3 The bonus system

The *prima* and the *premio* are the two main forms of productivity bonus in Cuba, and can (somewhat unhelpfully) be translated as the 'award' and the 'prize'. Introduced at around the same time – *primas* in 1979 and *premios* in 1981 – the main difference between them is that the former are paid out individually to workers, while the latter are distributed collectively and include management. *Primas* are met from the wage bill, while *premios* are a reward paid out of profits. They share the same basic objective, to enhance productivity and efficiency. Both are governed by general regulations, and both may be subject to additional specific regulations at industry or even enterprise level.

To receive either form of bonus depends on satisfying an 'indicator' or 'indicators' (never more than three) and specific 'conditions' (again, not more than three), which can range from fulfilling output targets for production and productivity, to meeting deadlines, making improvements in quality, or achieving savings in raw materials and energy. In other words, conditions and indicators can be either quantitative or qualitative. There is also a 'principal condition' – even if all the indicators are met, there will be no bonus payment if it is not satisfied.

These indicators and conditions can be targeted quite sharply to attack specific weaknesses in the production system, or to promote priorities as a result of changes in the broader economic context. For instance, if the wear and tear on equipment is considered excessive, it can be listed among the conditions, or even made a 'primary condition' so that no bonuses will be paid without improvements in this specific area. Equally the incentive system can be used to give priority to objectives such as saving fuel, or the more intensive use of machinery.

3.2.4 *Primas* ('Awards')[14]

The more widespread form of bonus is the *prima*, which is applied individually to workers linked directly to production. *Prima* rates vary widely and depend on the priority which is attached to each specific activity, but in no case exceed 30 per cent of basic wages.

For example, in the poultry farming sector, *primas* for manual workers vary from 7 to 20 per cent of basic rates and the main indicator is the cost of animal feed per unit of production. Here the 20 per cent ceiling applies to workers in the feeding or hatching sections, while for workers in the stock replenishment department the maximum is smaller, at 15 per cent. For non-manual poultry workers, meanwhile, whose right to *primas* is also conditional on the efficient use of feed, they range between 5 and 15 per cent of basic rates.

A portion of the *prima* is paid simply for achieving the plan target.

In livestock state farms, where workers are eligible for bonuses up to 30 per cent of their basic rates, the first 10 per cent is paid for meeting the target. This is paid out of a *prima* fund, which is provided for the budget agreed with the planning authorities. However, the *prima* fund can be enlarged through savings on wages and material costs, of which 50 and 30 per cent, respectively, are put aside for this purpose. It is this which creates the reserves for the extra earnings workers can receive by exceeding the targets or 'overfulfilling' the plan, as it is generally described.

Ideally, the bonus is paid as soon as possible after the work is performed to maximise the incentive effect. In practice, however, the frequency of bonus payments varies considerably. Sugar workers tend to receive their *primas* fortnightly or monthly, while on vegetable farms the bonuses are sometimes only distributed once the harvest has been gathered. Where enterprises do award bonuses for savings achieved during a portion of the year, they cannot later impose deductions if the grains failed to meet expectations over the year as a whole. Once a payment is made, it cannot be withdrawn.

The 'indicators' generally apply to the enterprise as a whole, while the 'conditions' apply to specific work processes. For instance, an 'indicator' could specify the volume of vegetable production required on a collective farm before the workers would become eligible for *prima* payments. In this example the 'condition' might regulate the quality of the tomatoes produced – if the 'indicators' are quantitative, the 'conditions' will be qualitative, and vice versa.

While *primas* are based on individual performance in principle, therefore, even workers with an excellent production record may be rendered ineligible to receive them, if, for example, one of the 'indicators' specifies a maximum energy consumption for the enterprise, which is then exceeded. In other cases it may not be possible to define an individual's contribution for technical reasons, in which case *primas* will be awarded on the basis of group or team performance.

In particular, where enterprises have adopted the 'permanent' (in agriculture) or 'special' production brigade system (in industry), the brigades are treated as a single unit by the enterprise in assessing their bonus awards (though they may operate their own individual bonus system within the brigade).

3.2.5 *Premios* ('Prizes')

As with *primas*, indicators and conditions are laid down which must be satisfied before the bonus is awarded, but since *premios* are based on the performance of the enterprise as a whole (or the new production brigades where these have been established) the conditions are applied at this level, and not to performance in particular work processes. But there is another condition which must be met before *premios* will be paid out – namely, the increase in labour productivity must be greater than the relative increase in average wages, including *primas*, since *premios* are paid out of profits.

They are paid out annually at the end of each financial year. The maximum is one month's salary. But up to 10 per cent of the *premio* fund may be kept aside for collective purposes, such as housing, clubs, child-care facilities, social amenities, sports, travel, welfare and recreation.

Both forms of bonus are a flexible instrument to promote productivity and efficient use of resources, but the incentive effect of the *prima* appears to be more direct. Not only are maximum rates higher (30 per cent against one month's salary per year) but *primas* are paid more frequently, and rates can be fixed as needed for specific operations and categories of workers. The fact that *primas* are individually calculated, whereas *premios* depend not only on the collective effort but also on the overall productivity increase exceeding the relative wage increase in a given year, also means that *primas* are a more dependable reward for individual effort.

On the other hand, whereas *primas* are available only to workers directly involved in the production process, the *premio* includes management staff. Since quality of management is often critical to key operations and overall performance, it is possible that resources disbursed as *premios* may have a more powerful economic effect.

Unfortunately, detailed analysis or raw data dealing with the economic impact of such incentives has not been published or made available. It is evident that indicators and conditions can be specified in such a way that the schemes become totally self-financing. By linking payments to specified improvements in productivity and savings, the result should be more than adequate to cover the extra outlay, and in fact it appears that most of the bonus schemes in operation do finance their own costs.

3.2.6 Moral incentives

Although the emphasis in the early 1970s swung towards 'material incentives', the Cuban leadership insisted that 'moral stimuli' must remain a cornerstone of the production process: 'It is impossible to substitute for . . . moral factors. We must not think for a minute that money is going to solve the problems that only consciousness will resolve.'[15]

Moral stimuli are naturally hard to evaluate in terms of their material results. They range from medals and diplomas, flags and other formal awards in recognition for outstanding effort and achievement, to more intangible stimuli such as exhortations and peer group pressures. What must be stressed, however, is that such pressures and rewards play a very prominent role in Cuban society today, despite the increasing reliance on material incentives, and are generally taken seriously. Lengthy television publicity is devoted nightly to the progress of selected work collectives or industries, and similar attentions are paid by the radio and printed press. The emphasis is dual; praise for results achieved, effort and 'attitude', and encouragement to achieve even more. Typically the focus for such publicity will be provided by a collective's formal pledge to overfulfil the plan by a stated amount in honour of, for example, a forthcoming anniversary.

Nor is it entirely possible to separate moral and material rewards, since the worker whose efforts are recognised in the form of an invitation to attend the annual 26 July celebrations, receives not only the prestige of a seat on the podium but also an expenses-paid mini-holiday. Longer holidays in the USSR and other socialist countries are also awarded to outstanding workers, particularly for achievements in the sugar harvest.

3.2.7 Socialist emulation

At the core of the system of moral stimuli is the institution of 'socialist emulation' whereby workers, collectives and enterprises are encouraged to compete with one another in the knowledge that, in doing so, they are increasing production overall. The system is organised under the auspices of the trade unions, and its structures are employed for selecting the 'most outstanding worker' of the month, quarter-year, half-year and year in every department of the state economy. Points are gained for time-keeping, output and 'attitude' – hours of voluntary labour were recently excluded from the calculation in a drive to make the system more directly output oriented – and the assessment is made by the trade union members themselves at the local level.

Probably the most important feature of the emulation system, in material terms, is that it generates the entitlement for workers to buy consumer goods – fans, air conditioners, washing machines, televisions, and so on – at cost price. A union is allotted a certain quantity of such items, which it makes available to the individual workplaces in its domain. The workers then apply for the right to purchase, and where demand exceeds supply a union committee puts forward recommendations based on a combination of emulation and need. The workers themselves discuss each recommendation and vote on it by a show of hands.

From workplace level, candidates are put forward to compete at the higher levels of emulation for honorific titles culminating in the highest awards of all – 'national work hero' and 'work hero of the Republic'. These carry indisputable prestige and are awarded by the highest political leadership.

3.2.8 Schools in the countryside

A different example of incentives to increased production is provided by attempts to link education with works in the schools in the countryside. Apart from bringing greater educational opportunities to the rural population itself, a majority of children from the cities now pass through boarding schools in the countryside, known as ESBECs (*Escuela Secundaria Básica en el Campo*) which are run on the 'work and study principle' – in other words, the pupils study in the morning and work in the fields in the afternoon, or vice versa.

Some fifty of these schools were founded in the year 1971 and by 1976 the system accounted for 31 per cent of total enrolment between the seventh and ninth grades (ages 13 to 15).[16] This integration of schooling and manual work aims to shape a positive attitude towards rural life and work in general, [17] and to emphasise the value of work and of farm work in particular. But it also fulfils an important economic function, since the students perform essential light labour on state farms (and in some cases cooperatives) during periods of peak activity. Farms pay the minimum agricultural wage for each pupil direct to the Ministry of Education, which in turn helps to cover the education budget. In 1976, the students earned for the ministry one-third of the budget.[18]

Typically, the ESBECs are associated with citrus farms where the work is not too arduous. The authors visited one such farm, the *Victoria de Girón*, where students from sixty-two secondary schools had been working in 1984, for which the Ministry of Education received 6 million *pesos* annually. The national operating costs of a secondary school of this kind are estimated at 200 000 *pesos*, from which it can be deduced that the students were earning about 50 per cent of the current costs of their education and upkeep.

3.3 PRICES AND DISTRIBUTION

3.3.1 The 1981 price reform

Before the mid-1970s, state farms were set production targets but little heed was paid to either production costs or quality. The SDPE brought in accounting methods which mean that all enterprises must take account of, and monitor, a series of indicators, enabling both managers and the ministries to take stock of performance.

The most important of these indicators is the cost per unit of production (*costo por peso de producción mercantil*) which functions as a profit rate for the enterprise. For example, a cost per unit of production of 0.80 means that every *peso* worth of production costs 0.80 *centavos* to produce, and implies a profit rate of something over 20 per cent.

However, the effectiveness of such a measure depends entirely on the realism of the prices which the enterprise receives. In 1980, prices had remained largely unchanged ever since the mid-1960s. The rectification of numerous anomalies was therefore a priority of the next year's price reform. Agricultural prices in particular were increased by a factor of 1.6 to 1.7 on average,[19] which had the unsurprising result of turning many loss-makers into profitable enterprises.

As a result of the 1981 price reform, State Planning Board (JUCEPLAN) officials told the authors, state farms should theoretically be able to achieve a 15 per cent profit, since the prices were fixed on the basis of costs of production plus 15 per cent. However, the input–output tables on which the calculations were based do not take into account differences in natural soil fertility and other regional factors. Nor, surprisingly, did the reform take account of the wage reform which accompanied it. Official agricultural producer prices were not adjusted to take account of the resultant cost increases. These also had a differential effect on different farms – for example, costs of production rose far more for tobacco, a labour-intensive crop, than for livestock.

In general, the state had made allowances for such problems by tolerating the continued existence of loss-making enterprises – and even creating material incentives for those that reduce their 'planned losses'. A tobacco farm visited by the authors was unable to show a profit despite reasonably good yields. From the documents of the Third Congress of the PCC it appears that the authorities are now determined to make the price system sufficiently realistic and flexible to resolve such problems.

3.3.2 The state procurement system (*acopio*)

Acopio, meaning 'collection', is the name applied to the nationwide system of procurement for all agricultural produce, and comprises a huge network of depots and vehicles. Procurement is compulsory for all production of sugar, coffee, tobacco and beef. Other crops may be retained for local consumption.

The state farms sell all their output to the State, except for the small proportion grown for the workers themselves (*autoconsumo*). Until the recent abolition of the small farmers' markets both the cooperative farmers and the individual growers were able to sell their excess produce – once they had met the production quotas agreed with the State – through these outlets. But following the abolition, all produce must be distributed through state channels: *acopio* in the case of most produce, and the Select Fruits Enterprises (*Empresas de Frutas Selectas*) primarily for high quality perishables for sale on the parallel markets or for special use (such as the tourist industry).

3.3.3 The rationing system

The rationing system, introduced in March 1962, was designed to ensure that everyone could obtain the necessary minimum of essential food items. However, it rapidly also became a tool of distributing scarce resources – that is, an instrument of strictly economic as much as socio-economic policy.

The range of items 'on' and 'off' the ration has varied considerably since the system was introduced. As articles have become more abundant they have been taken off the list. Eggs and fish, for example, were put on the 'free' market in the early 1970s. In other cases, rationing has continued to be applied for social reasons. Fresh milk, for example, is now relatively abundant in Cuba but remains available on the ration to particular categories (children, expectant mothers, etc.), at 0.25 *centavos* for one litre per head per day. Beyond that amount, like other consumers, they must pay 0.80 *centavos* a litre, and may buy as much as they wish.

Every household has its ration book or '*libreta*', listing all the items and quantities to which its members are entitled. Farm households, no matter how much food they grow for themselves, receive the same entitlements as everyone else. Table 3.2 gives the monthly ration of one adult. Children, expectant mothers and the elderly are entitled to special rations, as we have already seen, and extra provision is also made for people on special diets for medical reasons, such as diabetics.

3.3.4 The 'free' market

Apart from the subsidised food available on the ration, through *autoconsumo* sales and school and workplace canteens, there are two main sources for the Cuban consumer to acquire food; the 'free' market and the 'parallel' market; a third source, the private farmers' market, was disbanded in the middle of 1986. (The 'parallel market' and – when it existed – the private farmers' market have significantly undermined the importance of the 'black' market.)

The 'free' market is run by the state, using the same retail outlets as the rationing system. 'Free' goods can be distinguished by their label 'VL' (*venta libre*) – 'free sale'. This does not mean they are literally free, of course. It means they can be bought in unlimited quantities, depending on the depth of the purchaser's pocket.

Prices on the 'free' market are fixed by the State, and require an official announcement before they can be changed. Items include:

(1) At punitive prices, articles that may also be available cheaply but in very limited quantities on the ration, such as coffee, tobacco and strong alcoholic drinks (the latter not available on the ration).

(2) Standard items not available on the ration: beer, soft drinks, crackers, butter, yoghurt, fish, eggs and some 'instant' foods are among the many items sold exclusively on the 'free' market. These are either staples in abundant supply, or items that might be described as standard but non-staple.

(3) Staples available on the ration, when additional supplies permit. Rice and beans can often be bought on the free market, for example, but there may be prolonged periods when they are

TABLE 3.2   *The adult monthly ration, 1983*

	Quantity	*Price (pesos/lb)*	*Value (pesos)*
Rice	5 lb	0.24	1.20
Beans	20 oz	0.24	0.30
Oil	8 oz	0.40	0.20
Lard	1 lb	0.30	0.30
Sugar (refined)[1]	4 lb	0.14	0.56
Milk[2]	3 cans	0.30 (/can)	0.90
Coffee	4 oz	0.96	0.24
Meat[3]			
beef	1 lb 4 oz	0.65	0.81
chicken	1 lb 11 oz	0.70	1.18
Tomato sauce	1 can	0.25 (/can)	0.25
Salt	8 oz	0.03	0.02
Bath soap	1 bar	0.25 (/bar)	0.25
Laundry soap	1 bar	0.20 (/bar)	0.20
Detergent	7 oz	0.60	0.26
Cigarettes[4]	60	0.30 (/pack)	0.90
Cigars	4	0.15 (each)	0.60
Bread	15 lb	0.15 (each)	2.25
Subtotal			10.42
Other allocations (a typical sample)			
potatoes	6 lb	0.12	0.72
oranges	1 lb	0.08	0.08
tomatoes	3 lb	0.20	0.60
Subtotal			1.40
Total			11.82

[1] In the central provinces less processed food is available and an extra pound of sugar is distributed.

[2] Condensed/evaporated. The elderly receive six cans per month, children under 7 and expectant mothers are entitled to 1 litre of fresh bottled milk per person at 0.25 pesos.

[3] The meat ration in rural areas is slightly lower because there is more available off the ration. The figures given here assume an equal division of the entitlement for beef and chicken.

[4] Those becoming adults after 1978 have ceased to receive any tobacco entitlement.

SOURCE   Medea Benjamin *et al.*, *No free lunch: Food and revolution in Cuba* (San Francisco: Institute for Food and Development Policy, 1984).

only available on the ration or the pricier 'parallel market' system. When 'freely' available, rice and beans cost 0.90 *centavos* and 1.00 *pesos* per pound respectively compared to their ration price of 0.24 *centavos*.

3.3.5   The 'parallel' market

The parallel market covers a multitude of items and situations. Its central feature is that goods are sold at whatever price the State decides – mostly on the basis of supply and demand. Changes can be made without warning, which in practice means that parallel market prices for prized goods closely mirror the unofficial 'black market' price – a factor which has helped to push the black market in food onto the sidelines.

Some of the goods sold within the parallel market system are not especially costly. In particular, fruit and vegetables sold through special state markets or *agromercados* have variable prices depending on the supply and the season, but are generally cheap and often low in quality. Prestige shops may sell some of the same items at a far higher price but have to export quality. Generally prices on the parallel market are set high enough to ensure that there are no queues.

For the consumer, therefore, the parallel market offers a source of food to top up the ration and for special occasions. The authors observed that Cuban households bought relatively little of the rationed articles which were also available in the parallel markets.

3.3.6   The private farmers' market

Until recently a controversial component of the marketing system was provided by the *mercados campesinos* or peasant markets, where individual private farmers and cooperatives could sell their own produce – once they had met the state-agreed quota – at prices fixed essentially by supply and demand. First permitted in 1981, the private farmers' markets, the only avowedly capitalist creation of the Cuban revolution, were temporarily closed in 1982 amid accusations against intermediaries and speculators taking advantage of the system, and finally disbanded following a decision adopted at the second assembly of cooperatives, in May 1986. In the view of President Castro they would leave behind 'a great lesson, much damage and who knows how many millionaires'. [20]

In Chapter 5, we shall return to the private farmers' markets briefly, to examine them from the producers' point of view. But despite their demise there is no doubt that the experience raises crucial issues, so far unresolved, about the supply and availability of high quality food, especially perishables, to the population of the cities.

The fact that prices were extraordinarily steep in the private farmers' markets underlines the nature of the problem. Here, as nowhere else, it was possible to overhear an exasperated consumer, confronted with vegetable bananas (plantains) selling at over 1 *peso* each, exclaim: 'This is the end of the peasant–worker alliance as far as I'm concerned!' Yet his very presence illustrated that alternative supplies – even for this endemic product of Cuba's rich soil – were by no means plentiful.

As far as the overall volume of farm produce bought and sold was concerned, the peasant markets were of only minor significance – in 1984 they accounted for less than 5 per cent of the total, according to ANAP. In 1985, sales amounted to 70 million *pesos* compared to 900 million *pesos* for foodstuffs sold in the parallel market (including industrial produce).

But in particular crops their contribution was disproportionately large. The best example may be that of garlic, a crucial ingredient of Cuban cuisine, for which the peasant markets were responsible, in the first half of that year, for 80.9 per cent of the total sold. To the typical Cuban household, enjoying a relatively large disposable income, and long accustomed to spending a high proportion of available cash on food – in dining out to supplement the meat ration, for example – the availability and quality of prized ingredients can easily outweigh considerations of price.

It should be remembered that the original purpose of the peasant markets was not only to expand production but above all to diversify output and increase quality. In other words, they were intended to help motivate not only the farmers themselves but all categories of workers, by offering them more, better quality and more diversified crops on which to spend their incomes.

From President Castro's comments on the closure of the peasant markets,[21] it is clear that the authorities recognise the challenge of replacing the service they offered through the state system, and specifically the parallel markets . However, the real impact of the elimination of these markets remains to be determined.

NOTES AND REFERENCES

1. *Informe del Comité Central del Partido Comunista de Cuba al primer congreso* (Havana: Editorial de Ciencias Sociales, 1978) pp. 111–16.
2. See S. Roca, 'Economic policy and institutional change in socialist Cuba', in *Journal of Economic Issues*, vol. 17, no. 2, 1983, pp. 405–13.
3. Communist Party of Cuba: *2nd Congress of the Communist Party of*

Cuba: Documents and Speeches (Havana: Political Publishers, 1981) pp. 175–6.

4. Tercer Congreso del Partido Comunista de Cuba: Informe Central al Tercer Congreso del Partido Comunista de Cuba (Havana: Editora Política, 1986) pp. 41–2.

5. Communist Party of Cuba: 2nd Congress of the Communist Party of Cuba, op. cit., pp. 175–6.

6. Ibid., pp. 177–8.

7. Ibid., pp. 176–7.

8. R. S. Fonte (ed.), *Aspectos Fundamentales de la economía nacional* (Havana: Editora Política, 1984) p. 93 and E. Yanez Gonzalez, 'El sistema de direccíon y planificación de la economía', in *Revista Interamericana de Planificación*, vol. 16, no. 61, 1982, p. 88.

9. Tercer Congreso del Partido Comunista de Cuba, 1986, op. cit. p. 55.

10. Tercer Congreso del Partido Comunista de Cuba: Résolution sur le perfectionnement du système de direction et de planification de l'économie (Havana, 1986).

11. A. R. Martín Sánchez, 'La política de empleo en Cuba', in *Revista Cubana de Derecho* (Havana) 12 (21), 1983, p. 139.

12. Comité Estatal de Estadísticas, *Censo de Población y Viviendas de 1981*, vol. 16, no. 1 (Havana, 1983) p. 203.

13. J. Acosta, *Teoría y práctica de los mecanismos de dirección de la economía de Cuba* (Havana: Editorial de Ciencias Sociales, 1982) pp. 315, 318.

14. See Comité Estatal de Trabajo y Seguridad Social: *Reglamento general de primas* (Havana, 1979).

15. Fidel Castro, *Discursos: Volume–II* (Havana: Editorial de Ciencias Sociales, 1976) p. 148.

16. Economic Commission for Latin America (ECLA): *Estilo de desarrollo y políticas sociales* (Mexico City: Siglo Veintiuno Editores, 1980) p. 97.

17. *Informe del Comité Central del Partido Comunista de Cuba al Primer Congreso*, op. cit., pp. 116–23.

18. ECLA, 1980, op. cit.

19. Interview with officials from JUCEPLAN, February 1985, Havana.

20. *Granma Semanal* (Havana: Central Committee of the Communist Party of Cuba) 1 June, 1986, pp. 3–4.

21. Ibid.

4 The State Farms

Between 1959 and 1963, the state farm grew from nothing to become the dominant sector of Cuban agriculture. But while the workers gained permanent guaranteed employment and greatly enhanced health care, educational opportunity and other social benefits, output failed to expand significantly under the new system.

By 1970 the state sector had swallowed an even greater proportion of agricultural land, and was receiving the lion's share of agricultural investment, but its performance remained stagnant, or in the case of sugar, unstable due in part to a chronic over-reliance on volunteer labour.

Today, the state farms account for 83 per cent of the land, 80 per cent of the agricultural workforce and 77.5 per cent of the farm sector's overall output.[1] These figures alone illustrate the overriding influence of the state farms within Cuban agriculture, while an economic record of steady growth indicates that they are at least holding their own in production terms.

4.1 POLICY DEVELOPMENTS

After 1970, the main thrust of policy-making was to undo the excesses of the Revolutionary Offensive, restoring material incentives and imposing, in a somewhat piecemeal fashion, stricter internal accounting methods.

It was only around the middle of the 1970s that major new initiatives began to emerge in state agriculture as part of the development of a comprehensive system of central planning. Chapter 3 looked at the development of new management and planning methods for the state economy as a whole, and provides much of the general background for themes which will be developed in the present chapter. However, there are a number of specific trends and initiatives of strict relevance to the state farms which should be highlighted at this point.

(i) **Concentration.** In the pursuit of economies of scale, state farms

TABLE 4.1   *Size and number of state farms, 1983*

	Number	*Size (ha)*[1]	*No. of workers*[1]
Sugar cane farms[2]	152	13 396	1 582
Livestock farms	161	18 989	1 137
Other state farms[3]	109	8 461	1 495
Total	422	14 255	1 390

[1] Averages.
[2] Includes 94 Agro-Industrial Complexes (CAIs).
[3] Excludes forestry and service enterprises.

SOURCE   Comité Estatal de Estadísticas, *Anuario Estadístico de Cuba 1983* (Havana, 1984) p. 193–4.

have been steadily amalgamated, to the extent that by 1983 their numbers had shrunk to 422 from almost three times that number a decade earlier.[2] This resulted in an average area of 14 255 hectares and an average workforce of 1390 (see Table 4.1). It is quite possible that this process of concentration will continue. Some agricultural experts believe the optimum size may be as high as 26 840 hectares (i.e. 2000 *caballerías*), although others prefer the present figure which is equivalent to just over 1000 *caballerías*.[3]

(ii) **Decentralisation.**   Alongside the restricted autonomy ushered in by the Economic Planning and Management System, the Permanent Production Brigades introduced from 1980 onwards by the Ministry of Agriculture represent a new form of workers' self-management and seem destined to spread throughout the state farm sector, including sugar.

(iii) **Industrialisation.**   In 1980, state farms in the sugar sector were transferred to the new Ministry of Sugar, since when they have been progressively combined with the sugar mills into Agro-Industrial Complexes or CAIs (*Complejos Agro-Industriales*). In other words, the farms and the sugar mills are treated as one administrative unit. It is envisaged that similar complexes will be established in other sectors, merging, in the first instance, fruit cultivation with canning and preserves.

(iv) **Mechanisation.**   Mechanisation has proceeded apace, particularly on the sugar farms where 64 per cent of the harvest was carried out mechanically during 1985–6.[4] In 1983, sugar farms in the state sector possessed an average of twenty combines. The sector as a whole had an average of 3.2 bulldozers per farm and 155 tractors.[5]

(v) **Self-provision of food (*autoconsumo*).** Since 1980 state farms have been encouraged to grow food for the farmworkers' themselves, both for use in the canteens and for home sales. Land is set aside if need be for this purpose and the necessary inputs are included in the annual plan.

(vi) **School labour.** As noted in the previous chapter, since 1970 the state has pursued a policy of building secondary schools in association with state farms. The pupils work and study in broadly equal measure. The system provides an important source of labour, especially for cultivating and harvesting citrus fruit.

4.1.1 How a state farm operates

There are four administrative levels in the state farm; at the top is the manager (*director*), with overall responsibility for the enterprise. The manager's duties, as specified in Decree No. 42 (which lays down the general rules for all state enterprises) are to:

> orient, direct and control the elaboration of the plan of the enter-
> prise with due regard to the figures and norms which have been set,
> to sign and pass on the project to the appropriate higher office for
> its approval and to take the necessary steps to guarantee the plan is
> implemented once it has been approved.[6]

Under the manager are five or six deputy managers (*sub-directores*), each in charge of an 'office' or *sub-dirección* with the technical, administrative and secretarial staff to oversee a particular area of the state farm's activity, namely: industry (in the case of sugar farms or CAIs); economics; agriculture (often called production); human resources; machinery; supplies; and (sometimes) irrigation.

Each deputy managerial office in turn controls a number of departments, and under them will come the sections. For example, the economics office will include a planning department, with sections for planning and statistics, and a finance department with a commercial section. The main areas of responsibility of each office are typically:

(1) *Economics*: accounting, finances, statistics, planning;

(2) *Agriculture* (or production): production, harvesting, pest control, animal sanitation (where relevant), irrigation (where no separate office exists);
(3) *Human Resources*: organisation, work and wages (*organización, trabajo y salarios*, often called simply OTS), social security, health and safety;
(4) *Machinery*: maintenance and repairs;
(5) *Supplies*: for production and services (the canteen, housing, workers' transport, etc).

The manager and deputy managers form the farm's Enterprise Council (*Consejo de Dirección* or *Consejo de Empresa*) which meets monthly to discuss the progress of the enterprise, formulate policy, and so on. The leaders of the trade union also attend these meetings as observers. However, the Council's functions are essentially advisory, and it is the manager who is ultimately in charge of running the enterprise.

Similarly, each *sub-dirección* may have its own administrative council, composed of the heads of department and the leaderships of the relevant trade union sections (*secciones sindicales*).

4.1.2   The organisation of production

Just as the other parts of the administration are divided into departments and sections, so the 'production' or 'agriculture' office has traditionally been divided into 'districts' (*distritos*) and 'lots' (*lotes*). This system is still fairly common. However, increasingly it is being superceded by a new form of organisation, the 'permanent production brigade' (*brigada permanente de producción*), a system which dramatically increases the flexible portion of workers' incomes through output-related rewards, while allowing far greater scope for workers' self-management.

Under the old system, each district of the farm operates its own administrative office which is a smaller version of the overall management structure of the state farm itself, with heads of economics, production, human resources, machinery, and supplies which operate in close liaison with the relevant departments of the central office, although they are directly answerable to the district manager.

The number of districts can vary considerably, depending on the type of farm. Agricultural farms tend to have between two and six districts, while livestock farms, which are generally larger, commonly have between four and eight. The size of each district also varies, and can be anywhere between 500 and 5000 hectares, although it tends to fall between 1500 and 3500 hectares.

The districts also control most of the labour and other resources used in their area. The authors found that numbers of workers ranged between 150 and about 600 per district, although this can increase considerably during the peak season; by a third on a partially mechanised sugar farm, and as much as 100 per cent on a labour-intensive tobacco farm.

The districts are in turn organised into a number of 'lots' – typically between four and eight to a district. The lot is the unit where the work is actually carried out.

4.1.3 Brigades under the old system

The workforce is organised into brigades of three kinds: the 'specialised', the 'complex', and the 'autonomous'. As their names suggest, the first concentrate on a particular kind of work, such as cane-cutting, whereas the second perform a variety of jobs such as soil preparation, seeding, fertilising, irrigating, weeding and harvesting. They are generally attached to a particular district – the one nearest their home – and may be attached to a particular lot.

The 'autonomous' brigades are specialist units that operate throughout the enterprise, performing such functions as repairs or construction. A machinery brigade, in charge of servicing and maintenance of equipment, also commonly operates at enterprise level, although with the steady accumulation of machinery and equipment on state farms, districts are increasingly forming their own local brigades for this purpose.

Generally, the workers in a particular brigade form a fairly stable group and work together throughout the year. But the structure is not entirely rigid. In some cases a brigade may be temporarily broken up and its members integrated into other brigades, or else various brigades might be merged to tackle an unusually labour-intensive task.

The brigade leader (*jefe de brigada*) allocates and supervises the daily tasks for each member, keeps a record of the work done, coordinates the transport and is responsible for discipline. He is elected by the brigade members themselves, and keeps in close contact with his immediate superiors at lot, district or state farm level, depending on the nature of the brigade and its work.

The brigades can be as small as six members or as large as about fifty. In general, brigades on non-sugar farms will have up to twenty-five members – although the figure may swell with temporary labour during the harvest period – while on sugar farms the cane-cutters' brigades or 'machete squads' (*pelotones de macheteros*) typically number thirty to thirty-eight and should not fall below sixteen or be above forty-eight.[7] Brigades operating with the mechanical harvester, meanwhile, range in size from about seventeen to thirty-three workers.[8]

4.1.4   The Permanent Production Brigades

The Permanent Production Brigades or *Brigadas Permanentes de Producción* (BPPs), unlike the traditional brigades on the state farms, are self-contained teams of workers and technicians with the full array of production targets and assigned resources needed to make them units of the national planning system in their own right. But how do they operate in practice?

The first nineteen BPPs were established in 1981 as an experiment involving a total of just nine state farms (although they continued to operate the traditional system as well). By 1983, however, thirteen farms had transferred fully to the new system, with some 159 BPPs between them and a total of 16 057 workers involved in the new scheme. The next year sixty-five state farms had been organised on the basis of the 'permanent brigade' system, with an average of sixteen BPPs per farm and seventy-six workers per BPP.[9] By mid-1985 a further eight farms had been switched over to the new system,[10] bringing the total to seventy-three out of a total of 406 state farms under the responsibility of MINAG. In some cases, a transitional structure has been adopted, forming what are known as 'direct lots' (*lotes directos*) to replace the old districts and lots.

During the experimental stage, none of the sugar farms was converted to the new system – the sugar sector was at the time undergoing its administrative merger of state farms and sugar mills to form integrated agro-industrial complexes (CAIs). Accordingly, it was only in 1985 that MINAZ started to implement the new brigade system within the CAIs, forming initially a total of 104 BPPs on seventeen out of its 143 CAIs.[11]

Although the new brigades integrate a variety of skills, there are divisions of labour between different brigades. Of the first 104 BPPs in the sugar sector, for example, only seventy-eight were direct production brigades, while seventeen were 'mixed' (*mixtas*) or 'complex' (*complejas*), providing such support services as machine repair, and nine devoted their efforts to *autoconsumo* production.

As a rule of thumb, the experts believe that in general agriculture a BPP should have between fifty and eighty members, and on the sugar farms between 100 and 130,[12] with seventy to 115 in the mechanised harvesting brigades and 100 to 140 in the manual cane-cutting brigades.[13] These guidelines appear to have been exceeded by a considerable margin on the first sugar farm BPPs, where the average works out at almost 200 members per brigade.

Figures provided by MINAZ show that of the 20 080 workers in sugar sector BPPs in early 1985, nearly nine out of ten were labourers. The next largest category was that of the technicians (5.95 per cent) with the remainder made up of administrative and service workers (2.14 per cent each) and management (0.85 per cent).

Although the territorial division of the state farm into lots and districts has disappeared wherever the new brigades have been established, the BPP is linked permanently – hence its name – to a particular area, and is expected to safeguard the fertility of the soil and prevent erosion and overexploitation of the area under its control.[14]

This area is smaller than the old 'district', which the specialists now regard as too large for effective management. Nevertheless, it can be very large. In the sugar farms, a BPP may be responsible for an area of between 100 and 200 *caballerías* (1342 to 2684 hectares),[15] although on the MINAG farms visited by the authors, brigades were responsible for hundreds rather than thousands of hectares.[16]

The organisational differences between the new system and the old are illustrated in Figure 4.1. Effectively the BPPs substitute entirely for the old districts, lots and brigades. On the ground this means that many administrative and technical personnel working at district level (or in some cases at the lot level) are integrated into the BPP and become more actively involved at the point of production. ('Before they didn't get their hands dirty. Now they do', it was put to the authors.)

The BPP, which tends to have a larger number of members than did the traditional brigade, is often subdivided into five or six work groups (*grupos de trabajo*, or *eslabones de trabajo* meaning literally 'work links'), and where necessary, the work group itself can be split up into 'teams'. Each work group has its own leader (*jefe de grupo*) or 'worker in charge' (*obrero con mando*) to plan, direct and control

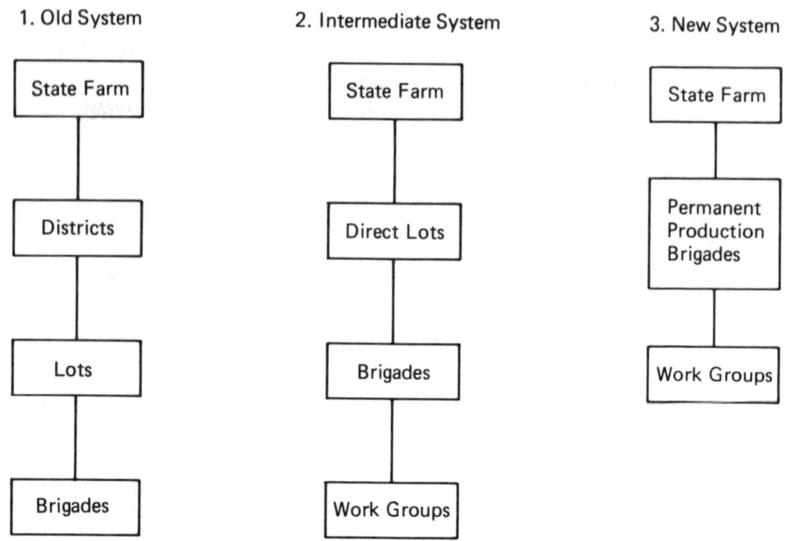

FIGURE 4.1   *Organisational chart of the state farm*

the group and where there are more than fifteen workers in the group the leader will not do fieldwork.

The BPP is led by the head of the brigade, who also chairs the Brigade Council (see Figure 4.2). The other members of the council are the heads of the work groups, the technical staff, workers selected as outstanding by the trade unions, and some trade union representatives. The council meets at least once a month.[17]

Unlike the old districts all the workers in a brigade attend the Production Assemblies – in the districts it is only the administration and the workers' representatives. The Communist Party, Young Communist League and trade union are all organised at the level of the brigade.

4.2   WORKER PARTICIPATION

4.2.1   The trade unions

The trade union is involved at almost all levels in the operation of the state farm. In the farms the authors visited the executive (*dirección*

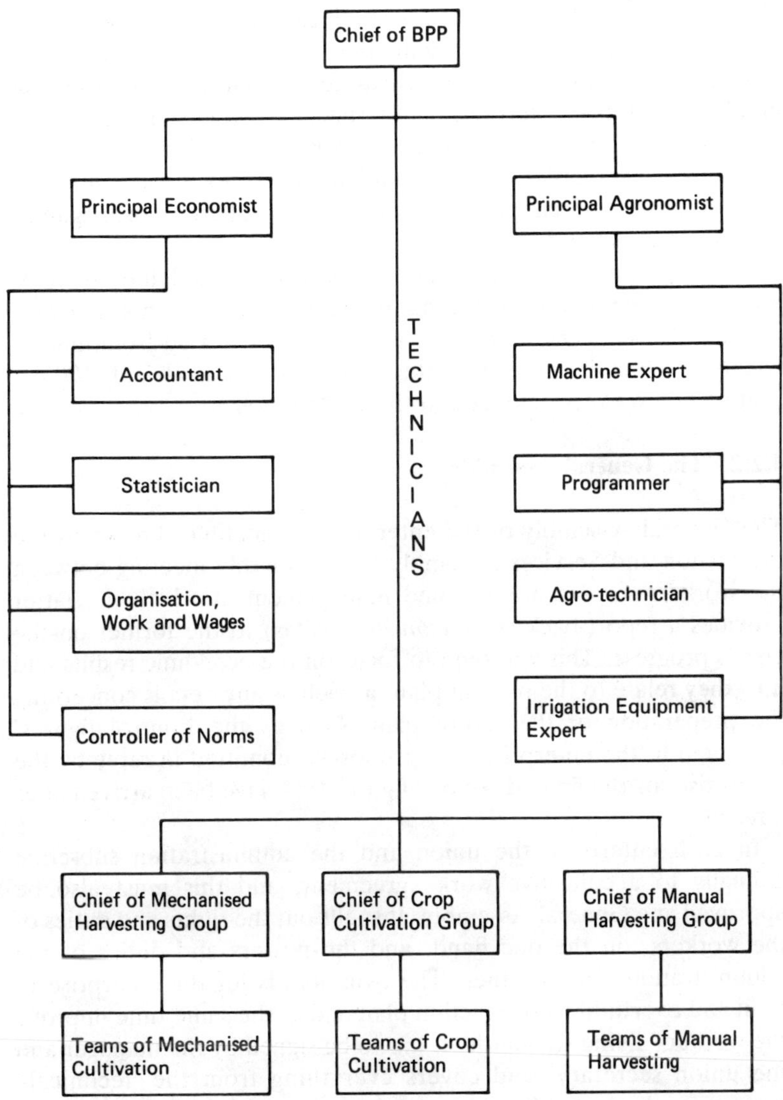

FIGURE 4.2 *Organisational chart of a Permanent Production Brigade (BPP) in a state farm (CAI)*

SOURCE R. González F. and M. Ramírez R., 'La estructura organizativa de la dirección en las brigadas integrales de producción de caña de azúcar', in *Economía y Desarrollo*, no. 83, 1984, p. 66.

sindical) typically had nine members, elected on a yearly basis by the union membership. One of them, the secretary, is a full-time employee of the union. The other eight, apart from working as normal employees of the enterprise, hold specific responsibilities such as organisation, finance, wages and work, production, health and safety, socialist emulation, social and labour issues (health, housing, *autoconsumo*, women, youth); or the general sphere of propaganda, education, sport and culture.

On the ground, the membership itself is divided into sections broadly corresponding to the administrative departments and production districts. The number of union sections varied from nine to twenty-seven in the state farms the authors visited. Invariably 100 per cent of the workers belonged to the trade union.

4.2.2 The General Assembly

The General Assembly of the enterprise – sometimes known as the Production and Services Assembly – is a monthly meeting between the workers' representatives and management at which the latter provides a report-back (*rendición de cuentas*) to the former on the farm's progress. This will tend to focus on the economic results and how they relate to the present plan, as well as any details concerning the preparation of the future plan, such as the 'control figures' presented to the enterprise, the proposals submitted in reply by the enterprise, or the final 'directive' figures that have been arrived at as a result.[18]

In each enterprise the union and the administration subscribe annually to a collective work agreement, and this must also be approved at a General Assembly. It spells out the rights and duties of the workers, on the one hand, and the powers and duties of the administration, on the other. The twin goal is for the enterprise to fulfil and overfulfil its production plan and at the same time improve the workers' living standards. It has to be signed by the manager and the union secretary, and covers everything from the 'technical–economic plan' and the organisation of work and wages to the 'observance of socialist legality', workers' cultural and educational development, health and safety at work, socialist emulation, women, sport and recreation.[19]

Officially, a quorum of 75 per cent is required for the assembly to proceed, and this is seemingly achieved with little difficulty. What is less clear, however, is the level of real participation that they achieve.

Certainly concern has been expressed at the dangers of merely formal discussion. In the words of one Cuban professor: 'The production and services assemblies must be carefully prepared in all respects, if they are not to become something formal where only cold figures are presented and the debate of the workers' fundamental problems is neglected.'[20]

4.2.3 The Representatives' Assemblies

All workers are expected to attend their Representatives' Assembly every three months. These are meetings of individual sections or 'work collectives' (*colectivos de trabajo*) at which issues of direct concern to the collective are discussed, such as production and work problems, attendance records, material and moral incentives, socialist emulation, or *autoconsumo*. The assembly elects representatives to the General Assembly and also receives a report on the decisions of the higher body. In principle, they act as a two-way transmission belt, conveying downwards the decisions and concerns of the higher instances, and the views and preoccupations of the workers in the opposite direction.

4.2.4 The Communist Party

As well as belonging to the trade union, some workers also belong to the Communist Party. On a state farm it is likely, but not automatic, that the manager will also be a Party member, along with other senior administrators. On one state farm about one in five of the permanent workforce was a Party member – there were 148 'full' and 'candidate' members (*militantes* and *aspirantes*). There were also 109 members of the Young Communist League or UJC (*Unión de Jóvenes Comunistas*). The party was organised into one committee and five cells (*núcleos*) while the UJC had five base committees.

4.2.5 Labour relations

The role of the trade unions in socialist societies is a contentious issue. In Cuba, the prevailing orthodoxy holds that such 'social contradictions' as exist are secondary to the common general interest, and are thus quite capable of resolution within the appropriate institutional channels. Consequently, the trade unions' role is quite as much to promote the general interest as to protect that of the workers.[21] As one official puts it, 'the point is to blend (*conjugar*) the individual interest with those of the collective and the state'.

At the same time, however, the political leadership has made it clear that it is keen to avoid 'domesticated trade union leaderships'[22] who fail to criticise superiors or to oppose their actions when these are arbitrary, unfair or counter-productive.

Such expressions of concern in themselves suggest that workers may on occasion be overpliant – whether to their own detriment or that of the enterprise and society as a whole – whenever, for example, a production assembly fails to generate genuine involvement and discussion. The authors' experience was not extensive enough to assess the scale of such problems. It was, however, pointed out that the workers have the right to request the ministry to replace unsatisfactory appointees, up to and including the manager. On one state farm the workers had recently removed two heads of brigade on their own initiative.

Whenever labour problems take the form of workers being punished for alleged breaches of discipline a clear legal framework is provided, in the form of a special Work Council (*Consejo de Trabajo*), elected by the workers themselves. This tribunal, since its members are not professional lawyers, receives technical advice from legal experts. It meets every three months or else as required to deal with appeals by workers against what they regard as unfair disciplinary measures taken against them. If either the worker or the administration is dissatisfied with the verdict then they have right of appeal to the municipal tribunal, then the all-professional provincial tribunal, and finally the national or supreme tribunal.

4.3 SELF-PROVISION OF FOOD (AUTOCONSUMO)

Workers' canteens are an important source of nutrition and sustenance for the Cuban population, whether in schools, urban or even rural workplaces. But it is only since 1980 that state farms have begun to supply their canteens from their own resources. Until then their canteens served food mainly brought in from outside. The new system is known as 'self-provision' or *autoconsumo*.

The general practice is for state farms to set aside a proportion of their land (between 3 and 9 per cent, to judge from the authors' visits to four sugar farms in 1985) to provide food for the workers. Although part of the land used for this purpose is made up of small, scattered plots unsuited to the basic crop (typically sugar), this should not give the impression that food production for *autoconsumo* is a marginal activity designed not to interfere with the main priority of the farm. In fact the *autoconsumo* area absorbs significant inputs, such as machines and fertiliser, and in some cases brigades will be devoted exclusively to producing food for themselves and their community.

The most obvious benefit of *autoconsumo*, as the authors were frequently reminded on their visits to state farms, has been the improvement in the quality and variety of food on offer in the canteens. Whatever is not used there is sold to the workers themselves, and unpublished data provided to the authors by the Cuban Workers' Confederation (CTC) for 1984 shows that as much of the *autoconsumo* production is taken home as is consumed at work.

In that year, from a sample of 382 state farms, 16 600 tonnes of tubers and vegetables, 2000 tonnes of rice, 1400 tonnes of grains and 2400 tonnes of meat were provided to canteens, compared to 14 900 tonnes of tubers and vegetables, 4200 tonnes of rice, 3800 tonnes of grains and 1200 tonnes of meat which were sold direct to workers.

Crops are selected for *autoconsumo* cultivation by the unions in consultation with the enterprise, enabling the provision of some staples that may be in short or irregular supply through other channels. As yet, however, this form of production plays only a minor role in total food production – 3 per cent in the case of rice, for example. But given the growing importance attached to this system of providing for the local population, it seems inevitable that its relative weight will tend to increase.

As an example, on the *Camilo Cienfuegos* sugar farm near Havana the equivalent of 63 *pesos* in food was sold to each worker in 1983 – equal to approximately five months' rations. The introduction of crops and livestock for *autoconsumo* not only helped to make up for crops in short supply, it also served:

(1) To rotate land. When the sugar plant is finished after five to six harvests, another crop such as beans should be grown in order to raise the nitrogen content of the soil.
(2) To balance labour requirements more evenly throughout the year.
(3) To help attract the few remaining private farmers in the area to integrate into the state farms.

Prices for *autoconsumo* produce are comparable to those paid in the ration system and the workers' canteens elsewhere in the country, and thus, it can be concluded, heavily subsidised, since only some transport costs are saved, while production costs can hardly be lower than those on the specialised units that provide the rest of the state-run food distribution system.

NOTES AND REFERENCES

1. All data refer to 1983 except for labour (1981). It is very likely that the data have changed only very marginally since then – if at all. Livestock data refer to *ganado vacuno*. Labour data are taken from República de Cuba, CEE, *Censo de Población y Viviendas de 1981: República de Cuba*, vol. XVI (2), 1983, (Havana: Oficina Nacional del Censo) p. 263. The remainder of the data are from República de Cuba, CEE, *Anuario Estadístico de Cuba 1983* (Havana, n.d.) pp. 104, 191, 194 and 215.
2. Juan Valdez P., 'El proceso de colectivización rural en Cuba', in *Estudios del Tercer Mundo*, vol. 3, no. 1, 1980, pp. 127–8.
3. E. Yañez González, 'El sistema de dirección y planificación de la economía (SDPE) y el perfeccionamiento organizativo de las empresas agropecuarias', in *Revista Interamericana de Planificación*, vol. 16, no. 61, 1982, p. 88.
4. *Granma Semanal*, 2 June 1986.
5. República de Cuba, Comité Estatal de Estadísticas, *Anuario Estadístico de Cuba 1983* (Havana, n.d.) p. 225.
6. Literal translation by authors. República de Cuba, Consejo de Ministros, *Reglamento General de la Empresa Estatal* (pamphlet, n.p., n.d.) p. 261.
7. Comité Estatal de Trabajo y Seguridad Social (CETSS), Resolución No. 529, Havana, 1980, p. 1.
8. Ibid., p. 4.
9. CTC, *Documentos sobre la Organización de Brigadas de Nuevo Tipo, basadas en los principios del Cálculo Económico Interno, de los diferentes sectores y ramas de la economía del país* (Havana: CTC, 1985) pp. 39, 40.
10. Interview with officials from CETSS.
11. J. López, 'Las brigadas permanentes de producción en el sector agropecuario', in *Cuba Socialista*, vol. IV, no. 3, 1984, p. 106.
12. Ibid., p. 112.
13. Interview with CETSS officials.
14. CTC, op. cit., p. 46.
15. MINAZ-CETSS, *Consideraciones generales para la introducción de las Brigadas Permanentes de Producción en la actividad agrícola-cañera* (Havana, MINAZ, 1983) p. 22.
16. There are BPPs which have far less land like one high quality pig breeding BPP we visited which only had five *caballerías* or 67.1 hectares. But these are exceptions.

17. CTC, op. cit., p. 19.
18. República de Cuba, Consejo de Ministros, *Reglamento* . . ., op. cit., pp. 261–2.
19. R.S. Fonte (ed.), *Aspectos Fundamentales de la Economía Nacional* (Havana, Editora Política, 1984) p. 99
20. E. Hernández Gonzáles, 'Participación de los trabajadores en la dirección de la producción socialista', in *Revista Interamericana de Planificación*, vol. 16, no. 61, 1982, p. 36 (our translation).
21. O. D'Angelo Hernández, 'Problemas de la eficiencia social de la qestión de dirección', in *Economía y Desarrollo*, no. 69, 1982, pp. 48, 51.
22. Ibid., quoting from a speech by Raúl Castro, the second general secretary of the CCP published in *Granma*, 7 August 1979.

5 The Non-state Sector

5.1 THE COOPERATIVES

During the 1960s, while agriculture became increasingly polarised between the state farm and the individual private farm, little official interest was shown in establishing a middle ground. The revolutionary takeover had prompted several thousand peasant farmers to collectivise on their own initiative. But without official encouragement or special support their number had steadily dwindled, so that by the time production cooperatives received official blessing as a 'socialist form of agriculture' in the mid-1970s, only forty-three remained.

More restricted forms of mutualism among small farmers, such as the peasant associations (*asociaciones campesinas*) and the credit and service cooperatives (CCSs), had enjoyed greater official backing and by the mid-1970s these embraced almost the entire membership of the small farmers' association, ANAP. But the impact of such structures was limited, at least if measured against the Government's ambitions eventually to socialise farm production altogether.

Meanwhile, the earlier initiatives to attract private farmers into full participation in the state sector were running out of steam. The pressure on them to sell their holdings into the state sector had dropped in the 'cooling off' period following the Revolutionary Offensive, with such transfers running at a mere 1500 a year after 1970. By the time of the 1978 census there still existed 137 695 peasant farmers owning an average 12.6 hectares for a total of 1 736 816 hectares.[1] The schemes for indirect integration – the 'specialised' and 'integral' plans – had also diminished in impact, with the numbers involved falling by half between 1973 and 1977.[2]

On the other hand, pressures had accumulated within the private sector itself towards a greater socialisation of production. Farmers' children were leaving home in response to the new educational opportunities, and developing careers elsewhere, often outside agriculture altogether. This accentuated the labour shortage and meant there was no one to take over on retirement or death. Even if farmers were willing to sell their land to the State, there might be no state farm nearby; and private sale was prohibited by law. The scale on which the peasantry has subsequently embraced collectivisation illustrates that the pent-up need for a collective sector may have been greater than the Government itself realised.

Whether it was tardy in recognising such needs, unwilling to abandon the goal of nationalisation, or a combination of both, the Government was also determined not to act precipitately. In order for collectivisation to succeed it had to be backed by adequate resources, and by the mid-1970s the State felt that Cuba had reached a stage in its economic development where it could finance a major programme of mechanisation and investment in the peasant sector without jeopardising further investment in the state farm sector.

The first signs that government policy were to change came in a speech by Fidel Castro on the fifteenth anniversary of the first Agrarian Reform Law, in May 1974, when he announced that the Government would encourage the voluntary integration of peasants into collective farms. The existing path – integration into state farms – was to remain open. The other path was to be the creation of producer cooperatives.[3] The initiative was formalised at the First Congress of the Cuban Communist Party (PCC) in December 1975,[4] and in 1977 the Fifth Congress of ANAP endorsed the policy of creating Agricultural Production Cooperatives (CPAs). Shortly afterwards the first ones were established.[5]

At all times the principle of *voluntaridad* was strongly emphasised. No peasant would be coerced into joining the CPAs.

5.1.1 Growth of the cooperatives

The rapid progress of the CPAs can be followed in Table 5.1, in which it is possible to distinguish three phases. Between 1977 and 1979 the number, area and membership all grew rapidly; by the end of this period the average size of a CPA was 143.9 hectares and the average membership twenty-three. There followed a second phase up to 1982 when growth was accompanied by concentration as the average size of coops expanded.[6] Thereafter, the processes of consolidation and concentration have predominated, with total land area and membership growing more slowly while the overall number of CPAs has remained roughly stable, so that by 1984, for example, the average size had reached 766.1 hectares and the average membership was fifty-one.

TABLE 5.1 *Growth of the cooperative sector, 1977–84*

Date	May 1977[a]	Dec. 1979[b]	Dec. 1982[b]	Dec. 1984[c]
Total no. of cooperatives	44	725	1 416	1 414
Total land area (ha)	6 052	104 300	690 500	1 083 292[1]
Total membership	365	16 692	63 285	72 597
Average size (ha)	137.6	143.9	487.7	766.1[2]
Average membership	8.3	23.0	44.7	51.3

[1] Includes 95 034 hectares given in usufruct by the State.
[2] Includes average 67.2 hectares given in usufruct by the State.

SOURCES (a) J. Ramírez Cruz, 'El sector cooperativo en la agricultura cubana', in *Cuba Socialista*, no. 11, 1984, p. 6.
(b) Comité Estatal de Estadísticas, *Anuario estadístico de Cuba 1983* (Havana n.d.) p. 193.
(c) Authors' interview with ANAP officials, Havana, February 1985.

Both ANAP and the State, following feasibility studies by the Ministries of Agriculture (MINAG) or Sugar (MINAZ), must approve the creation of a CPA. But the official attitude varies considerably from region to region. In some areas there are more applications than the State is willing to support. It is keen not to see the creation of loss-making CPAs, mainly because of the dangers of disillusionment if too many CPAs are seen to fail. In other areas, on the other hand, ANAP is campaigning actively to convince reluctant farmers to collectivise.

As of 1981, 64 per cent of CPA land had been contributed by members, 12 per cent had been bought by the cooperatives, and 4 per cent came from 'other sources'. The remaining 20 per cent had been contributed by the State. Both to encourage the formation of cooperatives and to make better use of the land, state farms in many cases transferred underutilised areas to a cooperative which might be in a better position to exploit it. By 1985, however, the proportion of cooperative land donated by the State had fallen to 6 per cent.

5.1.2 What do they produce?

Whereas state farms supply the bulk of food for domestic consumption – milk, eggs and meat – as well as export crops like sugar and citrus, the cooperative sector is dominated by production of export crops. Table 5.2 shows that cooperatives whose main crop is either

TABLE 5.2   *Cooperatives analysed by principal activity, 1983*

	Number	Percentage of total land	Average size (hectares)	Average membership	Production costs[1] (pesos)
Sugar cane	441	40	845	74	0.67
Coffee	290	18	591	46	0.70
Livestock	194	13	629	na	0.73
Tobacco	230	12	507	67	0.97
Vegetables[2]	226	12	498	na	0.69
Others	91	5	516	na	na
Total	1472	100	637	56	0.70

[1] Cost per unit value of production.
[2] Includes root vegetables.

SOURCES   J. Ramírez Cruz, 'El sector cooperativo en la agricultura cubana', *Cuba Socialista*, vol. 4, no. 2, 1984, pp. 10–11; Comité Estatal de Estadísticas, *Anuario Estadístico de Cuba 1983* (Havana, n.d.) p. 193.

sugar cane, tobacco or coffee account for 70 per cent of all cooperative land – although this figure may overstate the situation, since it excludes secondary crops, while including coffee farms (18 per cent of coop land) much of whose area, being mountainous, may not be in actual production.

Above all it is sugar that predominates, whether in terms of numbers of farms (almost a third), percentage of land (40 per cent), average size (845 hectares, considerably more even than the livestock CPAs) or membership (an average of seventy-four, more even than labour-intensive tobacco CPAs).

Sugar cane cultivation also seems to be the most profitable activity in the cooperative sector, since it has the lowest cost per *peso* unit of production, although there are particular crops within the category of vegetables, such as tomatoes and cabbages, whose returns are even higher.

How do the cooperatives arrive at their production targets? The process is broadly similar to the way state farm output is planned. That is, the planning authorities – through MINAG or MINAZ – make a proposal which is then negotiated with the CPA before final agreement is reached. The most obvious difference is that ANAP also intervenes in these discussions as a mediator.

The output target determines the supplies of fertilisers, seeds, pesticides and other inputs that the CPA will receive. But whereas state farms that exceed their output targets are simply regarded as having 'overfulfilled the plan', the cooperative regards its target from the outset as a bare minimum, since any surplus can be sold to the peasant or parallel markets at higher prices than the rest.

It is thus in a cooperative's interest that state procurement targets for its produce should be modest and that the State should pledge generous inputs in return. Both the Government and ANAP are keen to foster the cooperative sector and so far this process does not appear to have generated significant tensions, since the cooperatives tend to receive very favourable terms. On the other hand, certain products are more profitable than others. On one CPA the authors were told that cost per *peso* of production was 0.77 *centavos* for potatoes, 0.64 *centavos* for onions, 0.34 for tomatoes and 0.22 for cabbages. In general, it appears that the authorities will resist pressures to increase quotas for the more 'profitable' items if they consider this would result in excess, but this can only limit the scope for CPAs to pursue maximum profits. It seems likely, in the light of the decisions passed in 1986 at the Third Congress of the Communist Party, that such anomalies will increasingly be tackled wherever possible by more flexible pricing policies.

5.1.3 Credits and capitalisation

The cooperatives enjoy privileged access to credits and machinery. Their credits are charged only 4 per cent interest, compared to 6 per cent for individual farmers, and they receive a disproportionate amount of the credit available. In 1981, for example, the CPAs obtained 58 per cent of credit to the non-state sector, at a time when they produced only 15 per cent of non-state agricultural production.[7]

In its campaign to promote the CPAs, the Government has made particular efforts to offer plentiful farm machinery at low prices on medium to long-term credits. Such investment credits have to be repaid in yearly quotas over five to fifteen years. Table 5.3 indicates the growth of machinery and equipment on cooperatives between 1977 and 1984. For example, in 1984, cooperatives specialising in sugar cane had on average more than five wheeled tractors and one combine harvester. In practice, however, there are wide variations – one large CPA had thirty-six tractors at this time, including three tracked vehicles and a bulldozer.

TABLE 5.3	*Equipment and machinery stocks in cooperatives, 1977–84*

	1977–82[1]	1983	1984
Combine harvesters (sugar)	213	393	485
Tractors (wheeled)	4120	5115	7397
Tractors (tracked)	305	na	640
Lorries	667	1007	1182
Mechanical grab-loaders (sugar)	324	518	650
Trailers	3738	4573	7025
Irrigation systems	1130	1177	4531[2]
Seed drills[3]	117		226
Fumigation machines			289
Ploughs	1983		2593
Harrows	1249		1531
Jeeps and pick-ups			239
Vans			46

[1] Only includes stock sold by the state to CPAs.
[2] Includes irrigation motors.
[3] Includes non-sugar combines.

SOURCES	*1977–82*	C. R. Rodríguez, *CPA: 100 preguntas y respuestas* (Havana: Editora Política, 1984) p. 34;

1983	J. Ramírez Cruz, 'El sector cooperativo en la agricultura cubana', *Cuba Socialista*, vol. 4, no. 2, 1984, p. 10;

1984	ANAP officials, interviewed by the authors, 22 February 1985, Havana.

5.2   ORGANISATION

It can be quite an upheaval when the fences come down, both literally and symbolically, and a group of neighbours join forces in a CPA. In the first place, it means that production itself is reorganised. In one CPA the authors visited, each farmer used to have three fields: one for pasture; one for sugar cane; and one for food crops. When they joined forces the valley land was left exclusively for sugar cane – making it easier to harvest mechanically – while the food crops were transferred to the higher land, where they also built a large cowshed. The reorganisation failed to boost output in the first year, but subsequent yields improved. Previously none of the farmers had a cane harvester. Subsequently they acquired two of them.

No less demanding is the challenge to the farmers of creating a collective structure to manage their joint affairs.

In the first years of the cooperative movement there was no legal framework governing the cooperatives' internal democratic principles, nor had the 'general statutes' (*estatutos modelos*) been established by ANAP, providing formal organisational guidelines for CPAs. Both these were finally adopted in the summer of 1982, at the People's Power National Assembly.[8] Nevertheless, the earlier experiences of the Agricultural Societies (*Sociedades Agropecuarias*)[9] provided a model for the new collectives, and given the extensive role of ANAP and the State in the formation of cooperatives there is no sign that those established before 1982 differed significantly from the following typical model shown in Figure 5.1.

All members of a CPA belong to the general assembly, the highest body of the collective. The assembly meets monthly and must have a quorum of three-quarters of the membership. Resolutions are passed on the basis of a simple majority except in respect of funds to be financed out of profits, when a two-thirds majority is required.

All the main targets, plans and policies are approved by the assembly: the economic plan, the investment plan, contracts, the financial budget, prices and quantities for *autoconsumo* distribution, and so on.

The management board (*Junta Directiva*) meets every fortnight and has a quorum of one-half-plus-one. It is elected in a secret, direct ballot by the members, and holds office for two years. The prescribed model has thirteen to fifteen members, including the chairman (*Presidente*), vice-chairman, and secretaries of organisation, production, finance, supplies and services, education and culture, and ideology. There are also three to five members called *vocales* who may stand in for absent members of the management board. In practice, however, these numbers may vary more widely. In one CPA the management board had fifteen members; in another there were eight *vocales*.

Some of the management board are full-time administrators. At one CPA (where the secretaries were known as heads or *jefes*) the chairman, head of production, head of supplies and services and the head of machinery (a non-standard appointment) only occasionally worked in the fields.

The CPAs also have auxiliary committees (*comisiones auxiliares*), covering such areas as control, work-norms, socialist emulation, technical development, and health and safety. They are answerable in some cases to the vice-chairman, to the management board in others, or to the membership as a whole. The work-norms committee

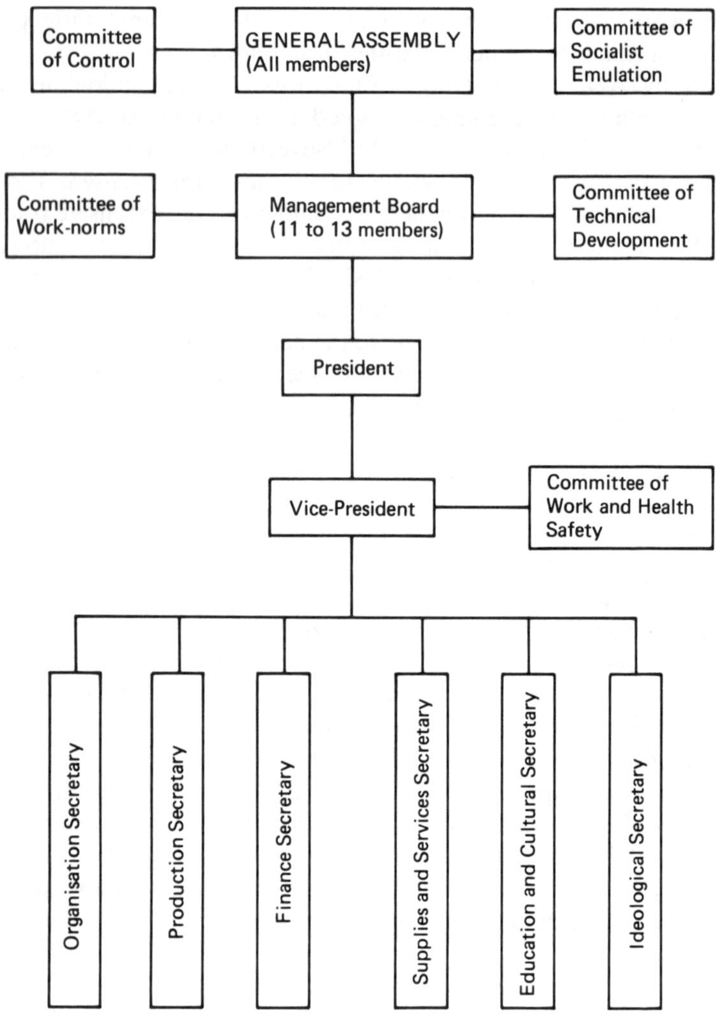

FIGURE 5.1   *Organisational chart of a cooperative (CPA)*

SOURCE   Elaborated by authors from field visits to CPAs, Cuba, February 1985 and ANAP: *Estatutos Modelos de Cooperativas de Producción Agropecuaria (CPA)* (Havana, 1980).

– comprising the chairman and three other members – is particularly influential,[10] since its decisions have immediate practical impact on the work and income of the cooperative members at large.

Although the management boards of the CPAs are sometimes criticised for taking too many decisions on their own without properly consulting and involving the rest of the membership,[11] the cooperatives can properly be characterised as self-managed collectives, since the members collectively own the land and other means of production, retain almost all their profits and in general run their own affairs democratically. Also, despite the mergers of recent years, CPAs are still relatively small, with, on average, a quarter of their members serving on the management board, and this alone enables the membership to retain a grasp of the collective's affairs and participate in its running.

5.2.1   Who are the members?

The CPAs have typically been formed among the members of existing credit and service cooperatives (CCSs). This means they may well already have experience of sharing irrigation equipment, machinery and even buildings – though the primary function of the CCSs is to organise credits and inputs – but until the CPA has been created, they have continued to farm individually. Indeed, during the first transition year following the formation of a producer collective it is by no means uncommon for the members to continue to take primary responsibility for 'their' portion of the common pool of land, and to receive the corresponding proceeds.

There are two categories of members: 'contributory members' (*socios aportadores*) who have contributed land, and 'non-contributory members' (*socios no-aportadores*) who have not – the latter almost invariably the relatives of the former. Neither category is likely to account for less than a third of the cooperative's membership. On a national scale, in 1981, 38 per cent of *cooperativistas* were contributory members.

Only a small proportion of CPA members are outsiders, that is, not related to other members of the cooperative. Generally, such people are brought in on the basis of specialised skills, and are accepted for a trial period of several months before being granted full membership of the collective. In one CPA visited by the authors, just five out of the 222 members came from outside. They included two male drivers for the coop's recently acquired combine harvesters and a female sugar cane agronomist.

It does appear, however, that in certain cases, especially rural areas which are fairly densely populated, ANAP has succeeded in convincing cooperatives to incorporate a larger proportion of landless outsiders than might otherwise have been done, resulting in some overmanning.[12]

5.2.2 Women

The female membership of the coops is very variable. Sometimes most of the wives are included in the membership lists, even if they work mainly at home. In other places, they are excluded from membership. The proportion of women on the four collective farms visited by the authors ranged from 15 to 44 per cent, although in no case did it appear that more than 13 per cent of those who worked throughout the year were women.

Women often organise themselves into a brigade of their own – this was the case on three of the four farms. The women's brigade may well be a 'mixed' brigade, that is, it would have various groups working in different areas. Typically the members of the women's brigade would be the part-timers, who would be expected to concentrate on what classically is seen as 'women's work': in the office, the canteen, and so on. But the other brigades are not entirely a male preserve and will include the minority of women who work full time.

5.2.3 Temporary workers and school labour

It may also be decided to hire outside labour on a seasonal basis. This is permitted, within the national labour legislation, only when the coop members' own labour is insufficient to guarantee full production during the peak period, and such an initiative must be approved by ANAP. All the CPAs visited by the authors took on outsiders for the harvest in this way, and in some cases for the planting season also. One such cooperative with a membership of 189 had taken on about 100 workers, of whom about a quarter were relatives, to pick potatoes for a fortnight. In some cases, cooperatives organise an exchange of labour between themselves.

Some of the seasonal workforce is local: relatives of the *cooperativistas*, pensioners, and so on. Other workers may be drawn from nearby villages, towns and even the large cities. One cooperative exchanged labour with a nearby CPA, but on a very limited scale.

Another significant source for labour is the schools. One cooperative had 150–180 secondary school children from the city working for about six hours a day during the harvest. In the mountain areas, where crops like coffee demand intensive labour for only a few weeks, school camps are particularly important in getting in the harvest.

The local schoolchildren, meanwhile, are also expected to learn about cultivation, and their schools are given special gardens which the pupils tend throughout the year, whether on a local state farm or a cooperative. Some 500 children from a local school worked for about three hours daily in the case of one cooperative visited by the authors.

5.2.4 Cooperative brigades

The members of the CPA are generally organised into brigades, each of which specialises in a particular activity, such as irrigation, agriculture, transport, machinery repairs, services or construction. A sugar cane coop will also have brigades for manual and mechanised harvesting, and its other agricultural brigades will also tend to be more specialised, with specific responsibility for such tasks as weeding, cultivation, sowing, fertilisation or, fumigation. As the work of some of these brigades only takes place at particular times of the year, at other times their members are integrated elsewhere, particularly during the harvest.

It is the responsibility of the management council (*consejo directivo*) to propose how the brigades are formed, and who should be their members. This is discussed and agreed at a general assembly of the coop. Each brigade has a 'number one' and often a 'number two' who work in close consultation with the secretaries of organisation and production to organise and distribute the work of the brigade.

Like the traditional brigades on the state farms, CPA brigades can divide into smaller work teams, and some members may even work on their own, performing a particular responsibility. They can also merge with other brigades to carry out tasks requiring more labour. In general, the membership of a brigade will remain fairly stable.

Production cooperatives are smaller than state farms and thus usually have fewer brigades. Three cooperatives visited by the authors had between eleven and thirteen brigades, and one had just six. But cooperative brigades are also characteristically smaller than their state farm counterparts — numbers generally varied between twelve and twenty, although they could be as low as six or as high as forty.

5.3   THE PAYMENT SYSTEM

How cooperative members are paid is a matter for each cooperative to decide, within the broad guidelines laid down in the CPA statutes,[13] but the general system is, in practice, fairly uniform. Benefits fall under four general headings:

advance wages (*anticipo*)
profit dividends
repayments for land or livestock contributions
farm produce (*autoconsumo*) at subsidised prices

Table 5.4 shows the breakdown of sources of income of cooperative members between 1979 and 1981.

TABLE 5.4   *Incomes of cooperative members, 1979–81*

	1979	*1980*	*1981*
Source of income (percentages)			
Wages	68.0	68.0	57.0
Profit dividends	23.0	22.0	30.0
Compensation payments	9.0	10.0	13.0
	100.0	100.0	100.0
Total income (million pesos)	6.5	14.6	37.2
Number of cooperatives	787	1027	1106

SOURCE   Banco Nacional de Cuba, *El crédito bancario en apoyo al desarrollo rural cooperativo* (Havana, 1982) pp. 15–16.

5.3.1   Wages and norms

Once the targets are agreed, it is the task of the CPA itself to decide how to meet, and preferably exceed, them. Although CPAs are not obliged to apply internal norms at all, the majority in practice do so. Initially, many CPAs find it convenient to use the work-norms applied on state farms, but if the state norms prove too easy to fulfil, they have an obvious incentive to set themselves more demanding norms.[14]

This is the job of the norm commission,[15] which typically selects three members of a brigade specialising in the relevant task. One will be a worker of low productivity, one of medium productivity and one of high productivity. They are asked to work for eight hours at their normal pace, after which the norm will be set at their average production. In fixing the norm the commission will also be aware of the national norm applied to state farms and also possibly the norms employed on neighbouring cooperatives.

Norms can be changed at the end of each year in the light of experience, and they should therefore become progressively more appropriate – the flexibility of the norm-fixing procedure on cooperatives makes them particularly responsive to those factors, whether human or material, which have a direct bearing on productivity. For example, if too many members have been able consistently to over-fulfil the norm it is likely that the commission will revise it upwards. However, it is not uncommon for members to challenge the norms, and indeed the lower the norm, the higher the advance payment (*anticipo*) an individual will receive for the same output. The individual worker's interest is thus to some extent posed against the collective interest in raising norms as high as possible in order to maximise productivity and profits. In general, it seems the prevailing direction of norms in the first years has been upwards.

5.3.2 Distribution of profits

Since cooperative profitability can vary widely between one farm, region or sector and another, there is an equally wide variety in the range of material rewards on offer to members. Nevertheless, ANAP and the Government are careful to provide a framework for the distribution of profits, if only to guard against the temptation to share out rewards at the expense of investment.

The net profits, where they exist, are usually distributed as follows: between 40 and 50 per cent is distributed individually to members; a further 25 to 30 per cent is spent on repaying members who contributed land and capital; 10 to 15 per cent is set aside for investment; 10 per cent for culture, sport and recreation, and 5 per cent for social services.[16]

In some cases the members also set up a current account or *fondo de medios de rotación* to reduce reliance on yearly credits from the National Bank which must be repaid at 4 per cent interest.[17]

The 50 per cent or so which the membership receives directly is paid out at the end of the financial year. Where the members pay themselves their regular wages as piece rates (the work-norm system) the profits are shared out in line with the wages they have received for the period in question. Otherwise, it is according to the number of days worked.[18] In 1981, profit dividends accounted for 30 per cent of CPA members' overall income.

5.3.3   Repayments

Of the cooperatives visited by the authors, members contributions on entry ranged widely, from an average of just over half a *caballería* (7 hectares) to just under 3 *caballerías* (38.5 hectares). Land, along with other assets such as livestock, machinery and implements, are carefully valued and their former owners receive full compensation over five to seven years, with between 25 and 30 per cent of the CPAs net profits typically set aside for this purpose.

This arrangement plays an important role in attracting individual farmers to join CPAs, and it seems the purchase price for land is generally higher than that offered by the State. Over the next decade, repayments should naturally decline to an insignificant proportion of *cooperativistas'* incomes, but in the early years as cooperative membership and land area expanded rapidly, the proportion of cooperative funds paid out in compensation to 'contributory members' tended to rise, from 9 per cent in 1979 to 13 per cent in 1981.

5.3.4   Autoconsumo

One of the main attractions of collectivisation for the small private farmer can be improved access to social facilities such as schools, health clinics, shops and other services. But moving to modern housing in a small community also means sacrificing the plot of land which has traditionally provided the Cuban peasant with many valued food items. Article 35 of Law No. 36 indeed prohibits coop members from raising privately owned animals except in exceptional, temporary circumstances, although wherever there is a backyard in rural Cuba it would be rare indeed for it not to house some hens and very probably a pig. This does not occur in the provinces of Havana and Havana city where domestic pigs are banned as a disease-control measure.[19]

What is permitted in Article 33 of the same law is for the cooperative to set aside land specifically for its members' own needs; the *autoconsumo* system. We have already come across *autoconsumo* on state farms, and there are not many significant differences here; as on state farms this land is worked collectively rather than individually, and what is not used in the canteen is sold to the workers at subsidised prices – usually the same as the state procurement prices, although this is a matter for the general assembly to decide.

It is worth noting that while private peasants only receive inputs for production contracted with the State for *acopio*, the cooperatives are entitled to inputs for *autoconsumo* production as well, so peasant farmers may actually gain improved access to local produce as a result of joining a coop. Entitlements to *autoconsumo* products are regulated by the general assembly on the basis of family size.

On the CPAs visited by the authors the proportion of land set aside for *autoconsumo* ranged between 1.7 per cent – where the cooperative's main activity was in any case food production – and 12 per cent. A sugar cane CPA reserved 4.7 per cent of its land for *autoconsumo* production of vegetables and livestock.

5.4 THE SMALL PRIVATE FARMS

Only some 17 per cent of Cuban farmland remains in the non-state sector, and of this, more than two-thirds has been amalgamated into cooperatives. The small private farms thus represent a distinct minority within agriculture today – and a sector which, the signs are, will continue to decline; officials anticipate that by the end of the decade only 5 to 10 per cent of non-state land will be cultivated by individual peasants.

This book has already explored the evolution of state and cooperative agriculture. The history of the private farms is, in a sense, the mirror image of that process. The agrarian reform process saw all private lands reduced to an effective maximum of 5 *caballerías* (67.1 hectares), expropriating the large landowners and, in its second phase, the medium capitalist farmers. This was accompanied by the distribution of land titles to more than 100 000 peasants. But subsequent years saw the continued expansion of the state sector with the sale of private farmland on a significant scale. And from 1977, the rise of the cooperative sector, analysed in the first part of the present chapter, has reduced the private farms to a point where ultimate extinction appears virtually inevitable.

Surrounded by a planned economy, the private farmers have had limited room for manoeuvre. They depend on the state for credits, supplies and outlets. Except in the recently closed peasant markets, they had no legal scope for fixing prices. To all intents and purposes, they depend on a regime which openly regards them as an 'inferior' form of agriculture.

Yet relations between the State and the private farm sector remain eminently cordial. There is no sign that the authorities have systematically used such levers to coercive ends. Indeed, of all the factors hastening the decline of small private farming, it seems that educational opportunity is the most powerful. Small private farmers today are generally elderly. Their offspring only rarely choose to take over the lands on which they were born, and work them in the old style.

Nor is the economic challenge of private agriculture entirely over. As the peasant markets showed, the private farmer may not be able to compete with large-scale methods in the cultivation of sugar cane, but the quality of his fruit and vegetables remains unrivalled. Until the 'superior' forms of agriculture can perform to the same standards, it seems fair to assume that they will not entirely supplant the individual grower.

5.4.1   Who are the private farmers?

The private farms can be divided into two groups. Many of them are concentrated in relatively isolated areas, away from the state farms, primarily in the eastern half of the island. Such areas look physically similar to *minifundia* (smallholding) regions elsewhere in Latin America – each farmer grows a range of crops, and raises cattle and poultry making the household largely self-sufficient. However, families are generally small, since the children typically leave home in their early teens to attend secondary school, and usually go on to establish their own lives elsewhere.

There are also still a number of small private farms dotted throughout the country, wherever a peasant has chosen to resist the overtures to integrate his holding. Driving through the Cuban countryside one frequently sees a pocket of land, its owner tilling the soil with an ox-drawn plough, in the middle of a vast expanse of state or cooperative farmland being worked by tractors and harvesters.

Private farmers receive credits, technical assistance and inputs from the state, channelled through ANAP and the Credit and Service Cooperatives (CCSs), of which they are almost all members. In the early years, quotas for production and inputs were agreed individually with each farmer, but nowadays ANAP and MINAG deal only with the CCSs.

The state procurement system, or *acopio*, has created a nationwide system of collection centres where local producers, including private farmers, bring their produce for sale at pre-established prices. If the farmer wishes to sell more than his quota he can do so directly to the State. If, on the other hand, he fails to meet his quotas, there is a system of penalties.

In general, the procurement quotas set by MINAG and ANAP are fixed relatively low, in comparison to those of the State and collective farms, as the authors were able to confirm in a visit to Holguín Province, in the east. Officials explained that since private farmers were not obliged to keep strict accounts, there was no record of the production figures of previous years. 'If we fix the quota much higher than the quota of the previous year, the farmer can always claim that the previous year's output barely covered the quota and that he could not meet a larger target,' explained one official. He also said that shortages of personnel meant that less qualified officials had to carry out the negotiations with the private farmers. In either case, it can be concluded that there is little official concern to elevate quotas for private farmers to the maximum possible extent. In all, the quota system provides a negotiable minimum, leaving farmers considerable scope to cultivate additional crops.

5.4.2 Private labour

The hiring of labour on private farms was abolished briefly in Havana province during the 1960s, but the 1970 census showed that there were still some 24 100 wage workers in the private farming sector in that year.[20] Although this was only 3 per cent of the total agricultural workforce, it implies that there was still a need for such labour, especially on the labour-intensive tobacco farms. The 1970s saw a growing official lenience towards the private hiring of labour, although a policy document issued towards the end of the decade, by explicitly confirming that temporary wage labour could be approved during the peak season,[21] indicated that permanent employment of this kind was not so approved.

Nevertheless, by the time of the 1981 census, whereas the number of private farmers had declined by 42 per cent since 1970, the number of wage workers they employed had shrunk to only 19 700 – or by 19 per cent.[22] The reason is almost certainly to be found in the growing labour shortages in the private sector, caused by the steady drift of the younger generation into other occupations. In other words, economic forces are pushing both ways; labour shortages directly increase demand for private wage labour, but indirectly reduce it by hastening the decline of the private farm sector as such. The second pressure appears from the statistics to have been dominant during the 1970s, and it seems likely that the overall reduction in private employment will continue.

5.4.3 The private farmers' markets

In Chapter 3, the private farmers' markets were described and some of the implications of their closure discussed from the consumers' point of view. But the Second National Meeting of Agricultural Production Cooperatives (CPAs), where the decision was taken in mid-May of 1986, also highlighted some important implications of the move for Cuban farming as a whole, and above all for the non-state sector which had enjoyed the exclusive right to these avowedly capitalist outlets.[23]

One reason strongly advanced for their closure was the continued prevalence of intermediaries, reaping unearned profits by buying produce from the peasants and reselling it to the workers at grossly inflated prices. This was also the reason given for their temporary closure in 1982, following which all sellers at the markets had to be officially licensed, requiring them to show not only their ANAP membership cards, but also proof that their obligations to the state procurement system had been met.

If such measures failed to block the speculators it could only mean that the speculators and profiteers were themselves card-carrying *Anapistas* (members of ANAP) – and in some cases cooperative leaders and members. On the one hand, therefore, the peasant markets were seen as a corrupting influence on the cooperatives and their members, and on the other hand, a source of excessive profits to individual private farmers which presented a major obstacle to the further expansion of the cooperatives. The extreme case was cited of a farmer allegedly earning some 400 *pesos* – a generous monthly salary – each *day*. And it is this which seems to have prompted the sweeping away of the peasant markets. 'Above all this phenomenon hampered the development of the cooperative movement itself . . . the decision which has been made will give a big boost to the cooperative movement in political and economic terms and in terms of morale.'[24]

The implications for the consumer of the closure of the peasant markets remain to be seen, with the clear risk that quality and availability of farm produce will be reduced. The state's success or failure in repleting this source of high quality food will presumably be reflected (or not) in black market activity. For the producers the likely implications are clearer: the implied clampdown on the wealthier private farmers must surely aid the expansion of the cooperatives, while simultaneously bringing the cooperatives themselves under tighter economic constraints.

NOTES AND REFERENCES

1. Comité Estatal de Estadísticas, *Cuba: Desarrollo económico y social durante el período 1958–1980* (Havana, 1981) p. 63.
2. J. I. Domínguez, *Cuba: Order and revolution* (Cambridge, Mass: Harvard University Press, 1978) p. 459.
3. O. Gómez, *De la finca individual a la cooperativa agropecuaria* (Havana, Editora Política, 1983) p. 66.
4. Departamento de Orientación Revolucionaria de Comité Central del Partido Comunista de Cuba, *Sobre la cuestión agraria y las relaciones con el campesinado: tesis y resolución* (Havana, 1976) pp. 44–6.
5. Adelfo Martín, *La ANAP: 20 Años de Trabajo* (Havana: n.p., 1982) p. 115–24.
6. R. Rodríguez, *CPA: 100 Preguntas y Respuestas* (Havana: Editora Política, 1983) pp. 76, 78.
7. Banco Nacional de Cuba, *El crédito bancario en apoyo al desarrollo rural cooperativo* (Havana, 1981) p. 2.
8. República de Cuba, Asamblea Nacional del Poder Popular, 'Ley No. 36, ley de cooperativas agropecuarias', *Gaceta Oficial*, No. 63, 24 August 1982.
9. ANAP, *Estatutos modelos de las cooperativas de producción agropecuaria* (CPA), (Havana, 1980).
10. Most of the above mentioned information has been taken from ANAP, *Estatutos . . .*, pp. 16–23.
11. I. Rojas, M. Ravenet and J. Hernández, 'La reforma agraria y el desarrollo rural en Cuba', *Economía y Desarrollo* (Havana) no. 83, 1984, pp. 147–8.
12. P. Peek, *From peasant to collective farmer: Cuba's third agrarian reform* (Geneva: ILO, mimeographed, 1986) p. 19.
13. ANAP, op. cit.
14. There exist dozens of books containing endless lists of norms for almost every conceivable task. It takes years to establish these thousands of

work-norms which are calculated by the State Committee of Work and Social Security (CETSS) and the Ministries of Agriculture (MINAGRI) and of Sugar (MINAZ).

15. O. Gómez, op. cit., p. 85.
16. ANAP, op. cit., p. 14.
17. Ibid., pp. 15–16.
18. O. Gómez, op. cit.
19. Field visits by the ILO Mission to various CPAs in Cuba, February 1985. See also P. Peek, op. cit., pp. 33–4.
20. Ibid., p. 23.
21. Comité Central del Partido Comunista de Cuba: *Sobre la cuestión agraria y las relaciones con el campesinado* (Havana, 1976) p. 51.
22. Peek, op. cit., p. 23.
23. *Granma Semanal*, 1 June 1986, pp. 3–4.
24. Ibid.

6 Labour and Development in Rural Cuba

How far has Cuban agriculture advanced since 1959? How have conditions changed for the rural workers and their dependants? What are the prospects for the future? These are the questions we shall examine in the coming chapter, looking first at social developments and amenities in the rural sector, then at trends within the labour force, including workers' incomes, and finally at the economic performance of the sector as a whole.

6.1 SOCIAL DEVELOPMENTS

In broad terms it can be said that social conditions in the countryside have improved immeasurably since the revolution came to power. A child born today in rural Cuba enjoys enviable prospects: guarantees of health care and education and prospects of security on reaching adulthood that could seem unattainable in many Third World societies. The fact is that Cuba's social investments, above all in health and education, are unusually large. In 1981, for example, the State spent US$140 per capita on education, compared to an average of US$16 for other countries in the lower–middle income bracket (as defined by the World Bank[1]). A similar commitment to health care – costing 15 per cent of the national budget in 1981, or approximately 55 *pesos* per inhabitant, compared to 3.5 *pesos* in 1959[2] – reduced infant mortality to less than fifteen deaths per 1000 live births by 1985 and increased average life expectancy to over 73 years. Such figures place Cuba among the developed nations in the world health league.

The Government's social policies and their often impressive consequences have been analysed at length in other studies. Let us therefore now look especially at those aspects of social provision that relate directly to the rural areas and the conditions of agricultural workers.

6.1.1   Education

Table 6.1 compares an age group that reached adulthood long before the revolution with an age group most of whose members were not born in 1959.

TABLE 6.1   *Educational attainment – contrasting two generations*[1]

| | Age in 1981 | |
Area	15–25	60 and above
Rural	14	89
Urban	5	61
Total	7	68

[1] Percentage of population not having completed primary school during childhood.

SOURCE   *Comité Estatal de Estadísticas, Censo de Población y Viviendas de 1981* (Havana, 1983) pp. 150, 153, 156.

The difference between the proportion of the two groups that completed primary schooling in their childhood shows clearly the very substantial improvement that has taken place in educational provision for Cuban children. It should be stressed that the table does not reflect the eventual educational attainments of the older generation, virtually all of whom acquired basic literacy through the 1960 literacy campaign and subsequent adult education programmes, and a large majority of whom had completed primary level education by the end of the 1970s, when the national 'Campaign for the Sixth Grade' was declared to have reached a successful conclusion. Such campaigns brought the official rate of illiteracy down to 1.9 per cent by 1981.[3]

The table also shows the gap in primary education attainment between the rural and urban areas – a gap that has narrowed from 28 percentage points for the older age group to 9 percentage points for the younger group.

The integration of urban and rural education has been powerfully promoted by the boarding school network of 'schools in the countryside' (ESBECS). We have already seen how the 'work and study' system on which they operate provides an important source of labour for the state farms, especially in light tasks and above all in citrus production. But this innovatory educational philosophy of the ESBECS also aims to transform attitudes to rural life and work in general.[4] Their role in mingling children from urban and rural backgrounds on a large scale can hardly be underestimated, even if the overall effects of this policy are difficult to quantify.

6.1.2 Health

Health programmes since 1959 have also strongly emphasised the rural areas. Almost from the beginning medical students – who, like teachers, are exempted from compulsory military service – have been required to spend at least two years in rural service after graduating.[5] The campaign in the 1960s to provide access to health treatment for the maximum number of the island's inhabitants also led to the creation of many strategically sited cottage hospitals and rural clinics. By the mid-1980s all hospitals had been transformed into fully equipped teaching hospitals, and provided with such facilities as intensive care units. Plans are under way to provide a doctor for every 200 families, working parallel to the existing network of clinics and hospitals, and the cooperatives are being given the priority as this 'family doctor' system develops.

On the state farms there is in all cases a medical post, and often a clinic staffed by a full-time doctor. Cooperatives also include, in most cases, at least a medical post. Treatment – except for prescription charges – is free.

The cost of health care on the state farms and cooperatives is completely covered by the Ministry of Public Health. On the *Valle de Peru* state farm the authors found a sixteen-bed clinic with laboratory and ambulance, employing thirty-three people and catering for 3120. They were told that the upkeep of the clinic had cost 120 000 *pesos* in 1984. The farm had not been required to fund any of this service.

6.1.3 Social security

Before the revolution only 30 per cent of the workforce was covered by social security legislation. But amid the sweeping reforms of the early 1960s all wage workers were given cover, and today virtually everyone, including private farmers, enjoy rights to some statutory benefits.

Wage workers on the state farms, like all state employees, are entitled to sickness and disability benefits and maternity leave. Pensions, to which men are entitled at the age of 60 and women at 55, are set at 50 per cent of average annual salary plus 1 per cent for each additional year of service after twenty-five years. Nevertheless, workers are permitted, and indeed encouraged, to continue working after they have reached retirement age.

Since there is no system of workers' contributions – except in the cooperatives – the entire cost of social security is borne by the State, which paid out an estimated average of 419 million *pesos* per year during the period 1959–80.[6] In 1978, for example, it was estimated that a third of all Cuban households were in receipt of benefits, with the monthly pension averaging 85 pesos.[7]

On the cooperatives, 3 per cent of each worker's share of the collective's earnings – the *anticipo* – goes into a social security fund. Official retirement age is five years later than on the state farms, namely 65 for men and 60 for women, and once again workers are encouraged to remain active as long as they can. The pensions are set at 40 per cent of average income – including both earnings (*anticipo*) and repayments on land and machinery contributed to the cooperat-ive (*utilidades*) – calculated over the five-year period when these earnings were at their highest level.

Private farmers, meanwhile, are not entitled to pension benefits under the social security programme, and the only financial protec-tion offered by the state to this sector relates primarily to sickness and death benefits for the farmers' households.[8] Nevertheless, if the farmer wishes to retire he can sell the land to the state or to a cooperative, for which he will receive the appropriate monthly pay-ments. In other words, the sale of private farms operates as a kind of retirement scheme for private farmers, and includes such provisions as access to the subsidised *autoconsumo* produce grown on the farm which acquires the land, and opportunities to work on an occasional basis.

From the state's point of view, evidently, this is an important mechanism in transforming agriculture to what it regards as superior forms of production.

6.1.4 Housing

Compared to the achievements in health and education, standards of housing in Cuba have made far less impressive advances. In many areas of the countryside, families still live in their *bohíos* – rustic huts with wooden walls, thatched roofs and dirt floors – just as they did before the revolution, even if inside those homes there is now almost invariably electricity, and more often than not a refrigerator and a television.[9] The television aerials sprouting from these bucolic dwellings are one of the features which most readily catch the eye of the visitor.

Most of those living in such houses are the families of the private farmers, since on the state farms and in most cooperatives the workers live in newly constructed brick and cement buildings, and the somewhat incongruous sight of a cluster of four or five-storey buildings in the middle of the countryside is another very characteristic feature of the modern Cuban landscape.

Several explanations arise for the relatively weak performance of the housing sector. First, supplies of construction materials have been limited, and priority has consistently been given to the construction of farms, factories, hospitals, schools and civil engineering projects. Second, the labour shortages, which were particularly acute up to the mid-1970s and remain a major problem in the rural areas, have clearly contributed to the housing problem. And third, housing is a relatively expensive service for the State to provide. Whereas the Government spends about 130 *pesos* per capita each year on education, and 55 *pesos* on health care, a single dwelling costs some 5000 *pesos* to construct, without counting the cost of maintenance and repairs.

At the same time, rural housing is generally in a better state than much of the urban housing, above all in the capital, Havana, where a low priority has been attached to building new dwellings and carrying out modernisation and repairs. This is partly from lack of resources and partly a deliberate attempt to deter the drift to the big city which plagues so many other nations of the Third World.

The Government devotes about 4 per cent of its budget to house building,[10] and much of the work is carried out by non-specialist workers on secondment from their ordinary jobs, who continue to receive their normal salary. These construction teams are known as the 'microbrigades'. In the past, the new housing stock was rented out to households by the State as it became available, but under the new Housing Law of 1985 all Cubans are to become owners of their homes, with the right to buy and sell, paying off the cost of their dwelling to the State over a period of fifteen or twenty years. Previously rent was subject to a ceiling of 10 per cent of income. Under the new law, the National Bank advances a credit to the home owner, with repayments subject to the same ceiling.

The National Bank also has a housing loan programme to provide construction credits to individual farmworkers and cooperative members – typically 5000 *pesos* repayable over fifteen years. Additional construction materials are also usually made available by the farm or coop, and the enterprise will also commonly form its own 'micro-brigade' to carry out the work.

It should be noted that the state farm or cooperative is not expected to fund the construction of housing for the workers. This is done by the State, through the People's Power system, which bears the financial responsibility for the building operation up to completion, at which point, under the new law, the incoming residents repay the local authorities using their loan from the National Bank.

6.1.5 Workplace amenities

Housing, education and health care, as we have seen, are not regarded as the financial responsibility of the state farm or coop, but are expected to be provided by the People's Power authorities or the appropriate ministries. Food supplies, meanwhile, are the joint responsibility of the State – through the national distribution network, the rationing system, and so on – and the farm itself, which sets aside a proportion of its land to provide fresh produce for the workers (*autoconsumo*). And even here, as we have argued, there is a hidden state subsidy, since the inputs needed for the *autoconsumo* crops are included in the planning arrangements without the State expecting any return on its 'investment'.

This means that the enterprises themselves are responsible for supplying only a limited range of benefits, such as children's nurseries, meeting rooms, vacation homes for the workers, and cultural, recreational and sporting activities.

On the cooperatives, 10 per cent of profits are generally channelled into the 'social and cultural fund' which is set aside for these purposes, while the arrangement on the state farms is more variable, depending on the type of crop grown and the size of the enterprise. In both cases, nevertheless, it is the level of profits that determines the size of the social fund.

As a result, the standard of the social amenities can vary considerably between one enterprise or coop and the next. Some units visited by the authors boasted a swimming pool, meeting hall, nursery, sports fields, televisions, a holiday home at some nearby beach and other benefits. Others had no more than a bare minimum. In general, it was apparent that festivities and collective amenities provided by the enterprise played a significant role in the workers' lives, and a considerable proportion of the workers' leisure time appeared to be spent at the pool, in the club, playing table tennis, and so on.

6.2   POPULATION AND LABOUR TRENDS

One important consequence of the radical improvements in Cuba's social provision and the sweeping changes in its economic life has been an equally radical change in the country's population profile, which is today more comparable to the developed than to the under-developed countries of the world.

In 1959, the population growth rate was running at 2.3 per cent per annum.[11] With the end of the insurrection, the birth rate accelerated remarkably, reaching an average of 30 per 1000 during the 1960s. In part, no doubt, this was a response to the end of hostilities and the greater climate of security which the advent of a popular government implied – although a decade which included such events as the attempted Bay of Pigs invasion and the October 1962 'missile crisis' can hardly be described as entirely uneventful. A more important factor may thus have been the improved incomes now enjoyed by broad sections of society. However, the higher birth rate, whatever its causes, was simultaneously offset by the departure from Cuba of some 215 000 people between 1959 and 1962,[12] so that the overall population growth continued at much the same, swift rate as before.

After the initial 'baby boom' the population growth rate slowed fairly dramatically, reaching about 1.1 per cent in the early 1970s and declining still further to 0.7 per cent in the period 1975–80.[13] With life expectancy rising and infant mortality falling, and a negligible rate of emigration, this was accounted for overwhelmingly by a fall in the birth rate. This occurred without any actively promoted birth control programme, either in the form of a publicity campaign or in the form of material incentives for parents to have smaller families – although previous moral constraints on contraception and abortion virtually disappeared in the new ideological climate, and both were made far more widely available by the expanding public health system.

This rather dramatic change should probably be attributed, first and foremost, to the island's prodigious public health achievements, including the near or total eradication of all the endemic infectious and poverty-related diseases which plagued pre-revolutionary Cuba, whose disappearance meant that parents could now confidently expect their children to survive them. Between 1970 and 1979, for example, infant mortality declined from 38.7 to 19.3 per 1000 live births. Full employment and the structural changes in the rural areas additionally relieved many of the social and economic pressures on parents to have large numbers of children.

A further important factor was the integration of women into the workforce, and the increasing school attendance rates and educational levels of future mothers – although even today there is concern at the number of pregnancies among teenage girls.

6.2.1   Urban shift?

The sweeping social transformations appear to have had a considerable impact on the distribution of the population between urban and rural areas. However, while some labour undoubtedly drifted off the land, the figures in Table 6.2 certainly exaggerate the extent of the shift. The proportion of the population living in rural areas apparently declined from 47 per cent in 1960 to 31 per cent in 1981. But in many cases this merely reflects a reclassification rather than physical relocation, since areas are defined as rural or urban accordingly to a set of criteria such as the range of public services and amenities locally available. As these have been extended to previously 'rural' communities, the latter have become officially 'urbanised'.

Thus between 1970 and 1981 some 250 000 rural dwellers became urban residents without moving home at all. The other side of the same coin is that the proportion of agricultural workers living in officially designated 'urban' areas increased from 23 per cent in 1970 to 32 per cent in 1981.[14]

In particular, the fact that Havana's population growth over the period of the revolution has been less than that of the island in general, and the other urban areas in particular,[15] points to an accumulation of population in the smaller urban centres, quite unlike the process of mass migration to the huge urban areas characteristic of most of the Third World over this period.

6.2.2   The labour force

If the rate of population growth fell sharply during the 1970s, the island's labour force statistics displayed almost precisely the opposite trend: there was a rapid expansion, as shown in Table 6.2. One might

TABLE 6.2 *Population and labour force, 1960–81*

A Total population					
	1960–70	*1970–81*	*1960*	*1970*	*1980*
	annual growth rate (%)			*thousands*	
All	2.3	1.1	6826	8569	9724
Rural	0.4	−1.1	3208	3342	3014
Proportion rural (%)			47	39	31
B Economically active population					
				thousands	
All	1.2	2.7	2318	2633	3541
Proportion rural (%)			39	37	27

SOURCES Comité Estatal de Estadísticas, *Censo de población y viviendas de 1981* (Havana, 1983), vol. XVI (1) pp. LV, LXVI, CCIX and vol. XVI (2), p. 263; and C. Mesa-Lago, *The labour force, employment, unemployment and underemployment in Cuba 1899–1970* (Beverly Hills: Sage Publications, 1972) pp. 22, 37; United Nations, *Demographic Yearbook 1970* (New York, 1971) table 5.

suppose this to have been the logical result of the demographic processes themselves, with those who were born in the 'baby boom' of the early 1960s beginning to look for jobs in the latter half of the 1970s. But in fact the entry of the new generation into the labour force was significantly delayed, for males at least, by the introduction in the mid-1960s of compulsory military service (three years within Cuba, or two outside). Further, the participation of those under 20 in the labour force dropped significantly between 1970 and 1981 as youngsters stayed progressively longer at school.[16]

At the same time, the participation of the over-60s in the labour force also fell, presumably in response to the introduction of comprehensive pension rights and other social security provisions. We are dealing specifically, therefore, with a very marked increase in the participation of the 20 to 60 age group in the labour force. Part of the explanation lies in the prevailing social and moral codes whereby work is considered not merely a right but a duty.

We have seen how from 1962 state farms took on the former seasonal workers – 73 000 had been given full time employment by 1975[17] – without always having sufficient work to occupy them throughout the year. Similar criteria applied throughout the economy, with jobs being created whether or not they might be productive. It must be supposed that many thousands who had effect- ively abandoned the labour force felt encouraged, or were legally compelled to return, and that further thousands formerly in unregis- tered 'twilight' occupations also moved back into formal employment.

While the absorption of labour for social reasons may have dis- guised an underlying surplus in some sectors, the economics of the countryside were dominated by the opposite problem: a chronic shortage of labour, which, as we have seen, necessitated the mobilis- ation of hundreds of thousands of volunteer cane-cutters at the height of the harvest season, reaching a peak in 1970. The challenge of subsequent years has accordingly been to level out the imbalances in the demand for labour through the mechanisation of agriculture – especially the sugar harvest; through the creation of year-round employment on the state farms (e.g. the *autoconsumo* system, de- scribed in Chapter 4); and, to some extent, through the institutional- isation of voluntary labour, including the establishment of schools in the countryside (ESBECS), whose pupils are responsible for much of the country's citrus cultivation (see Chapter 3).

6.2.3 Mechanisation

It has long been asserted by experts in the international sugar market that comprehensive mechanisation of the harvest is cost effective only when the value of manual labour rises above a certain level (such as US$1 per ton of cut cane). In Cuba, for the reasons we have seen, such calculations are less relevant, and the country has pursued such a consistent policy of introducing mechanical harvesters that it now accounts for over 60 per cent of the world total of these machines, producing more than 600 of them each year from its KTP plant in Holguín, eastern Cuba.

Already by 1970, 85 per cent of the loading and lifting operations had been mechanised through the introduction of grab-lifters (*alza- doras*), but very little of the harvest itself was carried out by mech- anical combine (only 1 per cent in 1970).

During the 1970s, as a result of domestic experimentation and research on the one hand, and foreign cooperation in the design of a harvester on the other, many of the technical problems were over- come, and as a result half the sugar cane harvest was carried out mechanically in the 1980–1 season, rising to 62 per cent in 1983–4. This has been reflected in a sharp decline in the number of manual cane-cutters or *macheteros*, from a high-point of 700 000 in the

TABLE 6.3   *Origin of manual cane-cutters, 1985*

Origin	Number	%
Workers recruited through mobilisation campaigns	22 000	32
Permanent workers of the sugar farms	20 000	29
Members of the Armed Forces	15 000	22
Private sugar farmers working on state or other private farms	12 000	16
Private sugar farmers working on their own farm	400	1
Total	69 400	100

NOTE   These rounded figures refer to the composition of this labour force on 10 February 1985.

SOURCE   Unpublished data provided to the authors by MINAZ.

1969–70 harvest or *zafra* to 153 000 in 1975–6, 100 000 in 1980–1, 80 000 in 1983–4 and about 70 000 in 1984–5. And, as Table 6.3 shows, only 22 000 of the 1985 manual workforce were mobilised workers.

Meanwhile, the 1970s also saw the complete mechanisation of cane-lifting operations in the fields, a 90 per cent mechanisation of ploughing in the sugar areas, and an increase in the proportion of cane cleaned mechanically from 25 to 53 per cent.

In non-cane cultivation, mechanisation also increased, though at a less spectacular pace. The number of tractors in use, for example, grew between 1970 and 1980 by 32 per cent from 51 600 to 68 300 (although it declined to 64 600 by 1982). Consumption of fertiliser grew by a similar amount (34 per cent) over the decade.

6.2.4   Unemployment

Table 6.4 can give only a general picture of unemployment trends, since it is drawn from a variety of different sources. It is worth noting, however, that the most recent data are official figures. Cuba is the only member country of the Council for Mutual Economic Assistance (CMEA) to publish data on the unemployment rate using United Nations criteria, in addition to the labour statistics prepared on the basis of CMEA criteria.[18]

TABLE 6.4   *Open unemployment, 1960–81*

Years	Unemployment (%)
1960	11.8
1965	6.5
1970	1.3
1975	3.1–4.5[1]
1981	3.4

[1] Alternative methods of estimating labour force growth employed by Brundenius produce a figure of 4.5 per cent for 1975. The lower figure seems more consistent with the overall trends and the steady growth in output between 1970 and 1981.

SOURCES For 1960–75 data, C. Mesa-Lago, *The economy of socialist Cuba: A two-decade appraisal* (Albuquerque: New Mexico Press, 1981) p. 122; 1975 data from C. Brundenius: *Revolutionary Cuba: The challenge of economic growth with equity* (Boulder: Westview Press, 1984) p. 135; 1981 data from Comité Estatal de Estadísticas, *Censo de Población y Viviendas de 1981* (Havana, 1983) vol. 16, no. 1, p. 102.

What the table unmistakably reflects is a substantial decline in unemployment over the 1960s followed by a modest rise in unemployment thereafter. The virtual elimination of joblessness by 1970 was the result of a number of trends already highlighted: above all the relatively slow growth of the labour force itself (1.2 per cent – see Table 6.2) and a determined policy of job creation.

The subsequent re-emergence of unemployment on a limited scale reflects the renewed expansion of the economically active population, the introduction of incentives for enterprises to save on labour costs, and mechanisation. Yet in the rural sector at least, mechanisation can hardly be said to have contributed to unemployment, since by and large the situation remains one of labour shortage rather than surplus. It is in the cities, in the backward areas of the east, and among graduates seeking a job to match their qualifications that the economy has chiefly failed to create employment opportunities to match demand.

In discussing the development of labour policy in Chapter 2, it was noted that the authorities have not sought, in recent years, to expand employment simply in order to absorb all potential workers, irrespective of their potential economic contribution, as was essentially the case in the 1960s. Indeed, they have stressed the need for enterprises to constrain the size of their workforce to match productive needs. With the rise in the economically active population, the consequent increase in unemployment has affected, above all, the young. The 3.4

per cent of all workers shown in Table 6.4 as unemployed in 1981 thus included, as we have already noted, 17.1 per cent of the economically active 17 to 19 year olds. This pattern, which is fairly new, reflects both the increased numbers of those now seeking work and the growing emphasis on restricting workforces to economic levels. While those affected are officially described as 'between jobs' rather than long-term unemployed, it is clear that, with the labour force expected to grow at 1.9 per cent per annum between now and the end of the century, the prospect of structural youth unemployment on a large scale poses an important challenge to the island's policy-makers.

6.2.5   Women in the workforce

Possibly the most marked development of all has been the incorporation of women into the workforce, with the proportion of female workers increasing from 13.1 per cent in 1960 to 23.8 per cent in 1970 and 31.3 per cent by 1981.[19] Few countries have witnessed such a sharp rise in such a short period, and the achievement must be attributed to the creation of jobs, on the one hand, plus the introduction of child-care and educational services to enable mothers to work.

Analysing what kinds of jobs have been taken by women is, unfortunately, complicated by the fact that official employment statistics distinguish between intellectual and physical work rather than providing a breakdown by status or remuneration: they show that in 1981, 56 per cent of women workers did intellectual work, against 24 per cent of men. But since this category ranges from research and management to simple desk work it tells us little about the social status of women's work, or comparative wage rates.

Nevertheless, from the breakdown of employment by sector, we can gain some insight into the differences between male and female occupations, illustrating not only that these are considerable, but also the considerable structural changes that occurred, at least during the 1970s.

It is noteworthy that in 1981 almost half of all working women were employed in services – essentially health and education – and that their participation in commerce declined very sharply (Table 6.5). It should be recalled that all small businesses were nationalised after 1968, and this may account for most of the fall.

In the rural areas, while male employment in agriculture has declined somewhat, that of women has risen significantly. This

TABLE 6.5   *Male and female employment by sector, 1970–81 (percentages)*

A Rural employment	1970		1981	
	Female	*Male*	*Female*	*Male*
Agriculture	24.1	67.3	35.9	61.9
Industry	16.3	8.3	13.0	9.0
Construction	0.4	3.6	1.7	6.9
Transport	0.4	2.6	1.1	3.1
Commerce	22.5	2.9	8.1	3.1
Social services[1]	32.8	13.5	35.9	12.5
Communications	0.6	0.1	0.3	0.2
Others	2.9	1.7	5.0	3.3
Total	100.0	100.0	100.0	100.0
B All employment				
Agriculture	8.1	34.9	10.2	27.9
Industry	21.1	20.1	17.7	19.4
Construction	0.7	7.2	3.1	11.5
Transport	0.9	6.6	2.8	7.8
Commerce	22.9	9.1	12.2	7.0
Social services[1]	41.9	19.5	49.2	22.3
Communications	1.4	0.4	1.1	0.7
Others	3.0	2.2	3.7	3.4
Total	100.0	100.0	100.0	100.0

[1] The 1981 census uses the category 'unproductive sector' rather than social services. Certain categories of workers may therefore have been transferred.

SOURCES   Comité Estatal de Estadísticas, *Censo de Población y Viviendas de 1981* (Havana, 1983) vol. 16, no. 2, pp. 683–96 and JUCEPLAN, *Censo de Población y Viviendas 1970* (Havana, 1972) pp. 349–54.

reflects the expansion in particular of fruit and vegetable cultivation, and also the large-scale introduction of battery farms for egg production, oriented in each case primarily to female employment.

At the same time, the figures in the above table may exaggerate the trend towards female employment in agriculture, since many of the former private small businesses and enterprises were taken over by the state farms following the 1968 nationalisation decree, and their workers were thus statistically transferred to the farming sector without necessarily changing their actual occupations.

6.2.6   The agricultural workforce

Chapters 4 and 5 traced the growth – or in the case of the private

TABLE 6.6   *Composition of the agricultural labour force, 1970–81*

	1970		1981		Annual growth rate (%)
	No. of workers	%	No. of workers	%	
State farms	495 073	63	598 762	76	1.7
Collective farms	1 800	–	30 223	4	25.6
Private farms					
Self-employed	235 001	30	135 926	17	−5.0
Wage workers	24 139	3	19 658	2	−1.9
Unpaid family					
workers	34 289	4	6 300	1	−15.4

NOTE   The distinction between private and state wage workers is not clear, especially for the 1970 figures. The data should thus be regarded as merely indicative.

SOURCES   Comité Estatal de Estadísticas, *Censo de Población y Viviendas de 1981* (Havana, 1983) vol. 16, no. 2, various tables; and JUCEPLAN, *Censo de Población y Viviendas 1970* (Havana, 1972) various tables.

farms, the decline – of the workforce in the three sectors that comprise Cuban agriculture. Table 6.6 summarises those trends.

In the 1960s, as we saw in Chapter 2, the agrarian reform process temporarily reversed the process of 'proletarianisation' that marked the pre-revolutionary period, with the distribution of land to the peasants effectively preventing their continued absorption into the wage-labour markets.

In the 1970s, and indeed from the mid-1960s onwards, the state farms began to absorb land from the private sector as small farmers retired or for other reasons sold off their holdings, and the trend towards wage work reasserted itself. Whereas private employment still accounted for 37 per cent of the total in 1970, it declined to only 24 per cent in 1981.

With the introduction of the cooperatives after 1977, the small private farm entered what appears to be an irreversible decline, whose beginnings are likewise reflected in Table 6.6. Since 1981, as described in Chapter 5, the incorporation of individual private farmers, their families and their wage-workers into the cooperatives has continued apace and nowadays less than 10 per cent of all agricultural workers are to be found in the peasant sector.

TABLE 6.7   *Estimates of distribution of personal income, 1962–78*
              (percentages)

Income group[1]	1962	1973	1978[2]
0–20	6.2	7.8	9.4
21–40	11.0	12.5	13.1
41–60	16.3	19.2	18.1
61–80	25.1	26.0	24.7
81–100	41.4	34.5	34.7
Gini coefficient[3]	0.35	0.28	0.26

[1] Expressed in percentages of the population, in ascending levels of income.
[2] Obtained by averaging the two different estimates provided in the source.
[3] Expressing the income-spread in a single figure: the higher the figure the greater the inequalities.

SOURCE   C. Brundenius, *Revolutionary Cuba: The challenge of economic growth with equity* (Boulder: Westview Press, 1984) pp. 114, 116.

6.3   INCOME DISTRIBUTION

We saw in Chapter 2 how a very sharp redistribution of income took place immediately following the 1959 revolution, with the very poor the main beneficiaries, and also how the trend towards greater equality continued throughout the 1960s, at a slower but still significant rate. Interestingly, this momentum was generally sustained during the 1970s, even though the original heavy emphasis on egalitarian policies had been diluted by the progressive introduction of material incentives from the beginning of the decade onwards.

Policies that might have been expected to promote greater inequalities included, for example, the creation of incentives to enterprises who saved on labour costs. And indeed some have argued that rising unemployment (see above) may have resulted in a more inegalitarian income pattern during the 1970s.[20]

Table 6.7, however, implies that income differences continued to level off. It is true that the position of the top 20 per cent hardly changed. Nevertheless, the income share of the poorest 40 per cent grew significantly, while the unemployed themselves, never more than 4 per cent of the workforce, were protected by social security benefits giving them an average 70 per cent of their previous wages.[21]

In the absence of clear statistical information, one can only guess at the trends in income distribution in more recent years. The widespread introduction of an individual bonus system for workers (the *prima*) should have encouraged greater equality, because those at the top end of the pay scale are excluded. On the other hand, basic pay differentials within occupational categories were widened by the wage reform of 1981 (see Chapter 3). It would probably be safe to assume that the overall pattern of income distribution in Cuba has now more or less stabilised.

Meanwhile, the growing availability of goods in the shops, including those sold at extremely high prices on the parallel market, mean that income differentials, whether they have marginally narrowed or widened, have certainly become more significant to workers in their capacity as consumers. It was noted in Chapter 2 that generalised scarcities in the 1960s and early 1970s largely undermined the relevance of differential incomes. So any greater availability of consumer items must logically have had the opposite effect, and in fact while many shortages persist the range of goods available to the consumer has certainly widened immeasurably since what are popularly remembered as the leanest years of the revolution, around 1970. Indeed, it has been an explicit concern of the Government to ensure that bonuses earned by greater effort can be realised in greater consumption, for otherwise they are meaningless and the incentive effect is lost.

6.3.1 Differences between state and non-state sectors

Are rural Cubans better off working on a state farm, working for themselves, or joining a cooperative? Unfortunately the data for the private sector – the cooperatives and the individual farmers – is too patchy to make any really conclusive comparisons, especially of cooperative incomes against those of the individual farmers.

The general conclusion to be drawn is that only the state farmworkers can be regarded as anything like a homogeneous group, as far as incomes are concerned. The peasant farmers include both some of the richest and some of the poorest members of Cuban society, and within the cooperatives a wide spread of income is also evident.

In 1985, the authors found that both cooperative members and small private farmers farming tobacco in western Cuba were earning above 300 *pesos* a month and sometimes as much as 400 *pesos*, a very respectable salary by Cuban standards. By contrast their counterparts cultivating beans in Holguín, eastern Cuba, were earning around 110 *pesos*.

Official figures for cooperative members' incomes published by the

National Bank in 1982 showed similar contrasts in monthly earnings: *cooperativistas* in mountain areas earned an average 42 *pesos* in 1979, 50 *pesos* in 1980 and 67 *pesos* in 1981. These compare with national averages for the same years of 175, 117 and 208 *pesos* respectively. It seems fair to assume that, on average, individual farmers have a lower income than the members of the cooperatives, partly because per capita farm size of the cooperatives is larger than that of their strictly private counterparts – and partly because they enjoy clear advantages in terms of state credits and other inputs.

What is quite clear, on the other hand, is that while state farm employees earn less than coop members and private farmers in general, the poorest state farm employees are considerably more secure than the poorest of both the private farmers and the *cooperativistas*. Table 6.8 shows that over the period 1979–81, coop members earned 23 per cent more than state farm-workers. On the other hand, we know that in 1981, the bottom grade of state farm labourer was earning basic wages of 82 *pesos* a month. Without even counting bonus payments – which may have brought the real take-home pay to around 100 *pesos* – this is considerably more than the 67 *pesos* that coop members in mountainous areas made on average that year.[22] Some peasants in remote regions must be assumed to have been earning even less, being little more than subsistence farmers; although since individual farmers as a group now constitute no more than 9 per cent of the rural workforce, the number of such cases must be extremely limited.

TABLE 6.8   *Incomes per worker on state farms and cooperatives, 1979–81*
             (Figures show average annual income in *pesos*)

	1979	1980	1981	Average
State farm worker[1] (A)	1418	1520	1923	1620
Coop member (B)	2100	1400	2500	2000
Ratio (B:A)	1.48	0.92	1.30	1.23

[1] Including bonuses.

SOURCES   Comité Estatal de Estadísticas, *Anuario Estadístico de Cuba 1983* (Havana, 1984) p. 108; and Banco Nacional de Cuba, *El crédito bancario en apoyo al desarrollo rural cooperativo* (Havana, 1982) p. 2.

6.3.2   Differences between town and countryside

If the income distribution pattern on a national scale has broadly stabilised, the same cannot yet be said for differences between urban and rural incomes. Agricultural workers gained more than their urban counterparts in the 1981 wage reform, with those at the bottom of the scale receiving an increase of 30 per cent. Further, the rapid mechanisation of the sugar harvest and other agricultural processes has had the effect of upgrading workers to higher wage scales more rapidly and in greater numbers in agriculture than in industry. As a result, average agricultural wages increased by 51 per cent between 1977 and 1983, compared to 25 per cent for average industrial wages.[23]

6.3.3   Regional differences

The Cuban authorities have consistently stressed the need for the more economically backward areas of the island to receive special attention: the principle of equal pay for equal work, even if rigorously and successfully applied, cannot produce equality of opportunity if one region enjoys more resources and infrastructure than another. And the fact is, the eastern regions of the island remain notably more backward in economic terms than the rest of the island. Within agriculture there are fewer state farms and a higher proportion of small peasant farmers, particularly in the mountainous regions. Industrial employment is also lower in the eastern provinces than in the rest of the country.[24]

From this one would expect significant regional differences in income, but at least as far as wages are concerned it appears that average earnings in the eastern provinces are only marginally lower than the national average: 2078 as against 2164 *pesos* in 1983, a difference of only 4 per cent.[25] This compares with a differential of 11 per cent in 1977, which suggests that in recent years the gap has been narrowing considerably.[26]

6.4   THE ECONOMIC PERFORMANCE

6.4.1   Growth patterns

The performance of the farming sector over the first quarter century of the revolution roughly mirrors the performance of the economy as a whole, even if, once again, there is a lack of reliable data on which to base detailed year-by-year comparisons.[27] However, it is safe to say that stagnation during the 1960s was followed by increasing output in the following years, as shown in Tables 6.9 and 6.10.

TABLE 6.9   *Growth of Cuban agriculture, 1961–83 – some estimates (percentage)*

Brundenius[1]	*1961–70*	*1970–81*	*1961–81*
Total agriculture	1.5	3.6	2.7
FAO[2]		*1970–83*	*1961/65–83*
Total agriculture		2.5	2.7
Per capita agriculture		1.2	1.2
Cuban statistical yearbook 1983[3]		*1970–83*	*1968–83*
Total agriculture		3.0	2.7

SOURCES   1. C. Brundenius, *Revolutionary Cuba: The challenge of economic growth with equity* (Boulder: Westview Press, 1984) tables A2.6, A2.8, A2.10 and pp. 148–54;
   2. Food and Agricultural Organisation, *FAO Production Yearbook* (Rome, 1976 and 1983 issues).
   3. Comité Estatal de Estadísticas, *Anuario Estadístico de Cuba* (Havana, 1983) various tables.

The Gross Domestic Product (GDP) increased rapidly from 1.5 per cent per annum in the 1960s to 6.7 per cent in the 1970s, rising further to nearly 7 per cent in the first half of the 1980s. Likewise, the growth of agricultural output rose from an annual rate of about 1.5 per cent in the 1960s to nearly 3.6 per cent in the 1970s.

Within this overall picture, Table 6.10 indicates that interesting structural changes have occurred, with sugar cane output expanding faster than agriculture as a whole during the 1960s, but then falling behind in the following decade.

The net result for the period 1961–81 was that sugar production grew slightly slower (2.0 per cent per annum) than agriculture at large (2.7 per cent).

Meanwhile, Cuba's other traditional export crops – tobacco, cocoa and coffee – actually declined over the period. State purchases, while by no means identical to total output in all cases, can certainly be taken as a close approximation as far as these particular crops are concerned, since sale outside the state's official network is illegal. This implies a falling trend of 2.1, 3.1 and 0.9 per cent per annum respectively for tobacco, cocoa and coffee (Table 6.11).

In compensation, food products have taken on a greater role than before, and within this category state procurement of animal products like pork, poultry, milk and eggs has increased fastest of all. Beef output (which declined 1.3 per cent a year between 1965 and 1983) has been the deliberate victim of a policy to give priority to milk production and other dairy products.

TABLE 6.10   *Growth and structural change in the Cuban economy,*
1961–81

A   Contribution to Gross Domestic Product – percentages

	1961	*1970*	*1981*
Agriculture[1]	*18.2*	*18.1*	*12.9*
Sugar	7.9	9.2	4.9
Other	10.3	8.9	8.0
Industry	*31.8*	*38.4*	*46.4*
Manufactures	24.4	29.7	30.7
Capital goods	1.6	2.5	6.6
Sugar and derivatives	4.7	4.8	3.0
Construction	5.2	5.7	13.0
Sugar – industry and agriculture	*12.6*	*4.0*	*7.9*
Total Material Production (TMP)	50.0	56.5	59.4
Gross Material Product (GMP)	82.2	79.9	73.2
Non-material Services (NMS)	17.8	20.1	26.8
Gross Domestic Product (GDP)	100.0	100.0	100.0

B   Average annual rate of growth – percentages

	1961–70	*1970–81*	*1961–81*
Agriculture[1]	*1.5*	*3.6*	*2.7*
Sugar	3.2	1.0	2.0
Other	0.0	5.8	3.1
Industry	*3.6*	*8.4*	*6.2*
Manufactures	3.6	7.0	5.5
Capital goods	6.5	15.5	11.5
Sugar and derivatives	1.8	2.2	2.0
Construction	2.4	14.2	8.9
Sugar – industry and agriculture	*2.7*	*1.4*	*2.0*
Total Material Production (TMP)	2.8	7.1	5.2
Gross Material Product (GMP)	0.2	5.9	3.3
Non-material Services (NMS)	2.9	9.3	6.4
Gross Domestic Product (GDP)	1.5	6.7	4.3

[1] Including forestry and fishing.

NOTE   Total Material Production is the gross value of agriculture, industry and construction. The Global Social Product is TMP plus the gross value of transport, communications and trade. The Gross Material Product is the GSP minus the value of intermediate inputs. Non-material Services are social services, administration, finance, commerce and defence. Gross Domestic Product is the total of GMP and NMS.

SOURCE   C. Brundenius, *Revolutionary Cuba: The challenge of economic growth with equity* (Boulder: Westview Press) 1984, p. 77.

TABLE 6.11   *Trends in state procurements – by suppliers (percentages)*

Crop	State's contribution 1980–3	1970–83 State	1970–83 Non-state	1970–83 All	1965–83 All
			Annual growth trends		
Sugar cane[1]	84.0	2.8	1.3	2.3	2.5
Potatoes	84.0	13.7	1.2	10.4	5.7
Malanga	67.0	18.2	3.6	11.1	3.0
Yucca	63.0	12.2	7.3	10.5	5.5
Tomatoes	43.0	4.7	13.0	8.6	5.0
Onions	54.0	6.4	–4.2	1.5	–0.3
Rice	94.0	2.4	5.5	2.6	9.3
Maize	62.0	–3.0	–5.0	–4.0	–4.4
Beans	48.0	1.6	–2.5	–0.4	–6.2
Citrus fruit	83.0	13.2	–0.4	9.4	6.4
Tobacco	38.0	6.8	–4.5	–1.2	–2.1[2]
Coffee[3]	61.0	6.1	–5.0	–1.1	–3.1[2]
Cocoa	33.0	12.0	–2.2	0.6	–0.9
Eggs	93.0			3.5	4.5
Milk	80.0			9.7	7.2
Poultry				8.2	6.8
Pork				13.4	12.7
Beef				–0.6	–1.3

[1] Data is total output.
[2] Data for period 1966–83.
[3] Figures were not available for the years 1965 and 1971–73.

SOURCE   Comité Estatal de Estadísticas, *Anuario Estadístico de Cuba* (Havana, 1972, 1976 and 1983 issues).

6.4.2   Exports: has Cuba managed to diversify?

It has been argued that the Cuban economy has experienced relatively little structural change over the past quarter-century, remaining heavily reliant on agriculture, and sugar in particular, in both production and trade.[28] Measured in current prices this is broadly true. In 1980–2 agriculture accounted for 86.3 per cent of export earnings – a proportion very similar to that before the revolution. There is some evidence that the country's orientation towards commodity exports has actually increased.[29]

However, a more accurate picture is obtained from measuring exports against production in terms of constant prices. And here we find that the ratio of exports to Gross Domestic Product has declined considerably, from 13.5 per cent in 1965 to 8.1 per cent in 1980,[30] while sugar's share of total exports fell from 88.3 per cent to 70.0 per cent over the same period.

A more convincing conclusion is thus, first, that Cuba's emphasis on commodity exports in general has decreased considerably and, second, that while sugar retains its grip over the export sector, its share has declined significantly.

The expansion of citrus production is one of the main factors in the diversification of the farming sector and its exports. During the 1980–5 period, the volume of production doubled.[31] At the same time, production for domestic consumption has also increased its relative share, with the output of root crops in particular – potatoes, yucca and *malanga* – all expanding consistently faster than the main export items.

Recently, the leading role of sugar specifically as an earner of convertible currency has been supplanted by the resale of Soviet oil, which the National Bank of Cuba has disclosed was worth more than US$400 million a year between 1983 and 1985, compared with around US$250 million for sugar.[32] This suggests that the damage caused by the long-term decline in world sugar prices has been considerably cushioned by this oil resale arrangement.

6.4.3 The cooperatives' performance

The government and ANAP are clearly pleased at the success of the collectivisation programme, not only in political terms, but also economically. Despite the upheavals inherent in reorganising production methods, most CPAs have quickly established themselves as profitable. Out of 761 established CPAs in 1982 (a further 655 of recent creation are not included in the figures), 674 collectives (88.6 per cent) showed a profit, with average cost per *peso* of production of .67 *centavos*. The remaining 87 coops showed a loss, consuming 1.28 *pesos* per *peso* of production.[33]

Another estimate, this time covering all CPAs, shows that the cost of production has tended to rise slowly during the 1980s, from 0.68 *centavos* in 1982 to 0.70 in 1983 and 0.77 in 1984.[34] According to ANAP this does not reflect declining efficiency, but rather the growing burden of repaying cooperative members for the land and equipment they contributed on entry. The eventual target is a production cost of 0.60 *centavos* per *peso* of production, which will obviously

TABLE 6.12   *Performance of the cooperatives,*[1] *1984*
(Figures in thousands of pesos except where stated.)

	All	Profit-makers	Loss-makers
Number of cooperatives	944	741	203
Value of production	156 738.3	141 227.2	15 511.1
Cost of production	120 653.1	103 020.4	17 632.7
Gross profits/losses:	36 085.2	38 206.8	−2 121.6
Other incomes	9 884.9	9 138.5	746.4
Other costs	10 953.7	9 711.6	−1 242.1
Taxes	839.1	839.1	0
Net profits/losses	34 177.3	36 794.6	−2 617.3
Average profits/losses (*pesos*)	36 205	49 655	−12 893
Cost per peso[2] (*pesos*)	0.77	0.73	1.14

[1] Results refer to only 944 out of a total of 1414 cooperatives. The accounts of the remainder were unavailable or had not been processed as of mid-February 1985.
[2] Cost of production divided by value of production.

SOURCE   ANAP *Typescript report submitted to the ILO delegation*, Havana, 18 February 1986, p. 2.

become easier to achieve as the repayment burden declines from the late 1980s onwards.

Table 6.12 nevertheless shows that the proportion of loss-making CPAs has tended to increase, from 11.4 per cent to 21.5 per cent between 1982 and 1984. Some reasons given for weak performances are that CPAs have taken on overambitious targets, failed to establish appropriate work norms for their members, and relied too heavily on time rates, whether for members or hired labour. There are also general shortages of technical skills in both production and administration: supervision, control, accountancy, etc.[35] ANAP officials acknowledge that this remains one of the main problems, not only in generating efficiency, but also in the creation of new CPAs.

6.4.4 Investment

Investment in agriculture rose rapidly after 1970, nearly tripling by 1983 (Table 6.13). Or to put this in a broader context, agricultural investment has consistently represented 20–25 per cent of Cuba's total investments since the beginning of the last decade. Where has the money been spent? The answer is, above all, irrigation, mechan-

TABLE 6.13 *Agricultural investment, 1970–83*

	1970	*1975*	*1980*	*1981–3*	*1970–80 (% increase)*
Total investment (millions of pesos, current values)	254	na	585	762	130
Irrigation (thousands of hectares)	520	593[1]	900[2]	990[3]	73
Fertiliser consumption (thousands of tonnes)	396	331	529	na	34
Tractors in use	51 600	54 851	68 300	64 600[3]	32

[1] 1974–6
[2] 1979
[3] 1981–2

SOURCES For investment data: *Anuario Estadístico de Cuba* various years. For data on irrigation, fertiliser consumption and tractors in use: *FAO Production Yearbooks* and *Country Tables*, various years.

isation, and land improvement: three areas of maximum priority for any agrarian country in the tropics.

The constant creation of new reservoirs has been reflected in a rapid and sustained increase in land under irrigation, of 73 per cent between 1960 and 1970 and 92 per cent between 1970 and 1982.

Much of the water has been dedicated to producing sugar: in 1975, 13 per cent of the land under sugar cultivation was irrigated (150 657 hectares) whereas by 1983 the proportion had reached nearly 29 per cent (345 801 hectares).

6.4.5 Productivity and yields

Two ways of measuring agricultural performance are to look at how much is produced per worker, on the one hand – productivity – and how much per hectare, on the other – yield.

In the state sector – the only area of agriculture for which such figures are readily available – the size of the workforce peaked around the years 1975–6. By 1983, seven years later, it had fallen back by as much as 13.4 per cent, due in large measure to the increasing mechanisation of the sugar harvest and other activities.

TABLE 6.14 *Labour productivity in state agriculture, 1971–83*

	1971	*1972*	*1973*	*1974*	*1975*	*1976*	*1977*	*1978*	*1979*	*1980*	*1981*	*1982*	*1983*
Workers (× 1000)[1]	604	637	670	675	685	685	636	640	620	624	619	616	593
Output per worker[1] (constant pesos × 1000)		1.43[2]			1.54	1.69	1.80	1.93	2.01	2.02	2.26	2.13	2.18

[1] Voluntary workers are not included.
[2] Average figure for the years 1971–4.

SOURCES Up to 1977 statistics on workers were taken from C. Brundenius, *Revolutionary Cuba: The challenge of economic growth with equity* (Boulder: Westview Press, 1984), and from 1978 from the *Anuario Estadístico de Cuba* 1983. Data on state agricultural production were taken from the *Anuario Estadístico de Cuba*, 1983.

Since this was also a period of increased output, it is not surprising that productivity should also have shown a considerable improvement, fastest of all between 1975 and 1979, but still appreciable in the years immediately before and after this period (Table 6.14).

As far as yields are concerned, official figures show an increase for state agriculture of less than 4 per cent per annum between 1975–7 and 1980–3. On a crop-by-crop basis, dividing the output by the area harvested, the yields increased in the state sector for all crops except tomatoes, reaching over 50 per cent over the period for beans and coffee (Table 6.15).

TABLE 6.15   *Yields on state farms 1975–7 and 1981–3 (selected crops)*

| | *tonnes harvested per hectare* | | |
	1975–7	*1981–3*	*% increase*
Tobacco	0.57	0.71	24.6
Coffee	0.13	0.20	53.8
Maize	0.77	0.78	1.3
Rice	2.58	3.53	36.8
Beans	0.30	0.47	56.7
Citrus	4.98	5.82	16.9
Potatoes	16.05	17.78	10.8
Malanga	8.70	11.15	28.2
Onions	4.09	5.45	33.3
Tomatoes	6.83	5.74	16.0
Sugar cane	45.80	54.80	19.7

SOURCE   *Anuario Estadístico de Cuba, 1983.*

Table 6.16 compares yields in both state and non-state agriculture during three periods: 1975–7, 1978–80 and 1981–3. Since these results were obtained by dividing output by the area planted rather than that harvested, the returns on tree crops such as coffee, citrus and other fruits, where plantations can show no harvest at all even after years of cultivation, would not have reflected the real situation and were accordingly excluded.

It will be noted that between 1975–7 and 1981–3, state yields declined for maize and onions, while non-state yields declined for tobacco, rice and onions. In all other categories yields improved. In the most recent period, non-state were higher than state yields for sugar, tobacco, potatoes, onions and tomatoes, but lower for maize, rice, beans and *malanga*. State farms improved their performance markedly in comparison to the collectives and private farms for

TABLE 6.16   *Yields in state and non-state farming, 1975–83. Figures show tonnes harvested per hectare*

| | 1975–7 | | | 1978–80 | | | 1981–3 | | |
Crop	State	Non-state	All	State	Non-state	All	State	Non-state	All
Sugar	45.80	53.70	47.20	52.77	58.77	53.73	54.80	62.00	56.07
Tobacco	0.47	0.70	0.64	0.43	0.54	0.50	0.60	0.66	0.64
Maize	0.66	0.11	0.36	0.64	0.22	0.38	0.58	0.32	0.44
Rice	2.72	2.88	2.73	3.10	2.39	3.05	3.47	2.75	3.37
Beans	0.21	0.09	0.15	0.27	0.11	0.18	0.35	0.22	0.29
Potatoes	12.54	12.97	12.65	16.85	18.85	17.15	16.68	19.14	17.01
Malanga	6.42	2.46	5.30	14.54	4.38	10.86	9.97	2.63	5.93
Onions	4.55	6.66	5.63	3.94	6.82	5.15	3.13	4.98	3.55
Tomatoes	6.13	7.14	6.70	6.10	6.84	6.49	6.33	8.24	7.43

SOURCE   *Anuario Estadístico de Cuba, 1983.*

tobacco, rice and *malanga*, while the opposite occurred with maize and potatoes.

6.4.6 Concluding remarks

Major advances have been made in Cuba over the past quarter of a century in education, health, social security, employment generation and elimination of absolute poverty. This has been made possible through institutional changes, relatively egalitarian income distribution and rapid growth of the economy since 1970. Progress has been less satisfactory with regard to housing and the economy faces a number of problems in efficient use of resources. The next chapter seeks to highlight the policies that have enabled Cuba to combine growth with equity and to identify some weak points and critical areas in the economy.

NOTES AND REFERENCES

1. United Nations Economic Commission for Latin America (ECLA), *Estudio acerca de la erradicación de la pobreza en Cuba* (Mexico City; mimeographed 1984) p. 81; and World Bank: *World Development Report, 1983* (Washington DC, 1983) p. 198.
2. ECLA, op. cit., p. 98.
3. Comité Estatal de Estadísticas (CEE): *Censo de población y viviendas de 1981*, vol. 16, no. 2 (Havana, 1983) p. 149.
4. F. Castro, *Informe del Comité Central del Partido Comunista de Cuba al Primer Congreso* (Havana: Editorial de Ciencias Sociales, 1978).
5. ECLA, op. cit., p. 95.
6. Ibid., p. 72.
7. Ibid.
8. Untitled and unpublished report prepared for the authors and provided by the Comité Estatal de Trabajo y Seguridad Social (Havana, 1985) p. 38.
9. CEE, op. cit., no. 2; and Tercer Congreso del Partido Comunista de Cuba, *Informe Central III Congreso del Partido Comunista de Cuba* (Havana: Editora Política, 1986).
10. ECLA, op. cit., p. 107.
11. C. Mesa-Lago, *The labour force, employment, unemployment and underemployment in Cuba, 1899–1970* (Beverly Hills: Sage Publications, 1972) p. 22.
12. Ibid., p. 41.
13. CEE, op. cit., no. 1, p. LX.
14. Ibid.
15. ECLA, *Cuba: Estilo de desarrollo y políticas sociales* (Mexico, Siglo XXI, 1980) p. 50.

16. CEE, op. cit., no. 2.
17. ECLA, op. cit., p. 129.
18. CEE, op. cit., no. 1, p. 201.
19. A. Farnos, F. González and R. Hernández, *The role of women and demographic change in Cuba* (Geneva: ILO, 1983) p. 17; and CEE, op. cit., no. 2.
20. C. Mesa-Lago, *The economy of socialist Cuba: A two-decade appraisal* (Albuquerque: University of New Mexico Press, 1981) chapter 7.
21. Unpublished report (see note no. 8 of this chapter).
22. Banco Nacional de Cuba, *El crédito bancario en apoyo al desarrollo rural cooperativo* (Havana, 1982) p. 27.
23. Comité Estatal de Estadísticas (CEE): *Anuario Estadístico de Cuba, 1983* (Havana, 1984) p. 107; and idem, *Anuario Estadístico de Cuba 1982* (Havana, 1983) p. 118.
24. CEE, op. cit., 1983, no. 1, p. LXVII.
25. CEE, op. cit., 1984, p. 108.
26. Comité Estatal de Estadísticas (CEE): *Anuario Estadístico de Cuba 1978* (Havana, 1979).
27. Data scarcity and reliability are extensively reviewed by C. Mesa-Lago and J. Perez-Lopez, *A study of Cuba's material product system, its conversion to the system of national accounts, and estimation of gross domestic product per capita and growth rates* (Washington, DC: World Bank, 1985).
28. Mesa-Lago, op. cit., 1981, p. 179.
29. Ibid., p. 183.
30. Claus Brundenius, *Revolutionary Cuba: The challenge of economic growth with equity* (Boulder, Col.: Westview Press, 1984) p. 75.
31. Tercer Congreso del Partido Comunista de Cuba, *Informe Central III Congreso del Partido Comunista de Cuba* (Havana: Editora Política, 1986) p. 6.
32. United Nations Industrial Development Organisation (UNIDO), *Cuba* (Industrial Development Review Series, Vienna, UNIDO, 1986) table 7, p. 22.
33. C. R. Rodríguez, *CPA: 100 preguntas y respuestas* (Havana: Editora Política, 1983) p. 73.
34. Authors' interview with ANAP officials, Havana, February 1985.
35. I. Rojas, M. Ravenet and J. Hernández, 'La reforma agraria y el desarrollo rural en Cuba', in *Economía y Desarrollo* (Havana, 1984) no. 83, pp. 147–8.

7 Cuban Experience in Rural Development: Some Concluding Observations

Cuba's post-revolutionary experience of development extending over more than a quarter of a century, offers many points of interest. Since 1959 a series of key institutional changes in the economy and society have taken place, accompanied by changing priorities in development strategy and in economic organisation and mechanisms. This final chapter summarises the main aspects of the island's economic and social performance, highlights its most distinctive features, and explores some underlying weaknesses and critical issues for the future.

7.1 ECONOMIC GROWTH AND STRUCTURAL CHANGE

In the twenty-six years since the revolution, the Cuban economy has grown at a moderately high rate, probably in the region of 5 per cent per annum. This growth, however, was unevenly distributed over the period: virtual stagnation in the 1960s was followed by quite exceptional expansion in the 1970s and 1980s. In terms of Gross Domestic Product (GDP), the annual rate of growth accelerated from 1.5 per cent in 1961–70 to 6.7 per cent in 1970–81 and about 7 per cent in 1980–5. As the rate of population growth declined over the period from 1.9 per cent per annum in 1959–70 to 1.5 per cent in 1970–9 and to around 1 per cent in the early 1980s, the spurt in growth in per capita output was even more impressive.

What are the reasons for the poor economic performance in the 1960s and a spectacular recovery in the 1970s and 1980s? It is easy to account for the poor performance in the first decade of the revolution. Briefly, the contributory factors included a massive outflow of professional, skilled personnel; major institutional changes resulting in the transfer to public ownership of the means of production in all sectors of the economy; the imposition of an economic boycott necessitating major reorientation in trade and capital flows; a substantial build-up in defence expenditure; sharp swings in development priorities, economic planning and management; and virtual abandonment of economic calculus and material incentives in the late 1960s. In the light of these factors it is perhaps surprising that output per head did not fall more during this period.

The sharp recovery and sustained economic growth over the past decade and a half are also the result of a multitude of factors. Among the more important ones may be mentioned the consolidation and institutionalisation of the new structures of production; the dramatic improvements in the skill profile of the labour force, in physical infrastructure – roads, transport, irrigation, and in machinery and equipment, as a result of massive investments undertaken in the 1960s and 1970s; the adoption of new policies in economic planning and management with emphasis on efficiency, material incentives, decentralisation and economic accounting; and last, but by no means least, the secure trade markets and stable and remunerative prices for exports and considerable financial and technical assistance offered by socialist countries, particularly the USSR.

Substantial economic growth has been accompanied by significant structural changes, at least if output is measured in constant prices. The share of agriculture in GDP went down from 18.2 to 12.9 per cent over the period 1961–81 and that of industry rose from 31.8 to 46.4 per cent. Within industry, the manufactures rose from 24.4 to 30.7 per cent and the capital goods sector from 1.6 to 6.6 per cent. The share of the sugar sector (sugar cane and sugar refining) fell from 12.6 to 7.9 per cent. Again measured in constant prices, the ratio of exports to GDP declined from 13.5 per cent in 1965 to 8.1 per cent in 1980, while that of sugar in total exports fell from 88 to 70 per cent over this period. Thus the economy became more diversified and less dependent on agriculture though exports continued to be dominated by sugar.

7.2 EMPLOYMENT PERFORMANCE

Prior to the revolution, open unemployment varied between 9 and 21 per cent according to the agricultural cycle. Unemployment declined rapidly in the 1960s to reach the low figure of 1.3 per cent in 1970. It rose somewhat in the 1970s and may have reached 4–5 per cent by

1979. The 1981 census estimated open unemployment at 3.4 per cent. What were the main factors behind the rapid elimination of open unemployment in the 1960s and the gradual emergence of 'labour surplus' in the 1970s?

The disappearance of unemployment was due primarily to the following five factors, not listed in any order of importance. Through the creation of state farms and cooperatives and allocation of land to sharecroppers, tenants and squatters, the agrarian reforms of 1959 and 1963 resulted in more secure and year-round employment for hundreds of thousands of agricultural workers. The result was not so much an increase in the number of workers as the elimination of seasonal unemployment for a significant proportion of the agricultural labour force. Indeed, through most of this period, the agricultural sector and especially the sugar crop was hampered by persistent labour shortages at harvest time, a problem met by a variety of special arrangements ranging from reliance on the armed forces to the mobilisation of hundreds of thousands of volunteer cane-cutters.

The second factor was the massive expansion of employment in the services sector, especially the health and education services. The early efforts to eliminate adult illiteracy, followed by the huge expansion of primary and secondary education and health services throughout the country, absorbed large numbers of workers. The third factor was the expansion of administration and the armed forces. Fourthly, the years immediately after the revolution were characterised by heavy emigration. Finally, the growth in secondary and tertiary education and the extension of social security schemes removed substantial numbers from the labour force.

To what extent did the expansion of employment represent a growth in productive employment and not merely the creation of artificial jobs to absorb the unemployed in state enterprises and bureaucracy? The right and obligation to work is a fundamental tenet of the Cuban Revolution. And it is well known that a socialist economy can absorb the unemployed without the constraints of profit-maximisation. It is, therefore, highly likely that some expansion in employment in the state sector in the 1960s was motivated by social considerations and could not be justified in purely economic terms.

Paradoxically, it is in the 1970s, with a marked acceleration in the growth of output, that there are some signs of the emergence of surplus labour. How does one explain the situation? It would seem that some of the factors at work in the earliest period ceased to be important; for instance, emigration became a negligible factor in the 1970s, becoming significant only in 1980. Similarly, employment momentum generated by mobilisation campaigns for literacy and the massive expansion of health and education services slowed down once the backlog had been made up and these services expanded at a more normal pace. The same may have been true of administration and defence.

On the other side, the normal growth in the labour force was reinforced by a big increase in the numbers of women seeking jobs. Perhaps the most important factor contributing to labour surplus was a determined drive by the Government in the 1970s to achieve greater efficiency and productivity in the economy. This comprised a series of measures including the introduction of economic accounting in enterprises, the linking of remuneration to output and greater reliance on incentive schemes. Their cumulative effect has been to 'squeeze' excess labour out of the economy. These measures have been reinforced by the accelerated drive for mechanisation, especially in agriculture. A dramatic index of the impact of mechanisation in sugar cane is the decline in the number of workers needed in the *zafra* (harvest), from 350 000 in 1969–70 to less than 69 000 in 1984–5. One result of the drive for greater efficiency is shown in large increases in labour productivity; in state agriculture, for example, productivity per worker rose by 5 per cent per annum between 1971–4 and 1980–3.

The reduction in the number of workers needed at the peak of the harvest bears witness to the effectiveness of policies to dampen the seasonal fluctuations in labour demand and ensure steadier, fuller employment for agricultural workers. Apart from the mechanisation of peak time work, other policy measures adopted at enterprise and regional levels included the diversification of agricultural production, an increase in cropping intensity through irrigation, the introduction of new varieties of seeds and the integration of non-agricultural activities such as construction.

7.3 EQUALITY, INCOME DISTRIBUTION AND LIVING STANDARDS

The achievement of equality was a passionately pursued goal of the early years and has continued to be one of the guiding principles of Cuban development policy. As far as incomes are concerned the trends towards equalisation have been particularly striking. One statistical measure, known as the Gini coefficient (where 0 represents complete equality and 1 complete inequality of income), shows a very sharp fall from 0.47 in 1958 to 0.35 in 1962, and a continuing decline to 0.28 in 1973 and 0.26 in 1978. This last figure is by international standards a highly egalitarian distribution of money income.

But incomes are only one indicator of the level and distribution of living standards. Especially in socialist countries, the 'social wage' – essentially health, education, housing and social security – is a significant component of real living standards. Almost from the beginning of the revolution, the Cuban government has sought to provide an increasing range of essential services free or at nominal rates to a widening segment of the population. An especially note-worthy aspect of this policy is the extension of such services to the rural areas. A few indices may convey the scale and range of this effort.

The provision of free basic health services throughout the country has resulted in an increase in life expectancy to 73 years in 1984 – a level comparable to the industrialised countries. The infant mortality rate first rose from 33.4 per 1000 in 1958 to 46.7 in the late 1960s, largely because of a more comprehensive registration of births, but then fell rapidly to 19.3 in 1979 and 15.0 in 1985 – again comparable to the figures in the industrialised countries. Per capita food avail-ability, which furthermore is distributed quite evenly, rose from 2552 calories in 1965 to 2867 in 1980 and 2929 in 1983. Serious malnutri-tion has been virtually eliminated.

In the field of education, the adult illiteracy rate was brought down from an estimated 21 per cent before the revolution to about 4 per cent in 1979. Primary education was made universal in the early years of the revolution and the proportion of students in secondary and higher education rose from 14 and 3.1 per cent in 1960 to 26 and 4.9 per cent in 1970 and further to 79 and 20.6 per cent respectively in 1980. These figures bring out the extraordinary progress made in secondary and higher education in the 1970s. A striking feature of the educational policy has been the establishment of a string of secondary schools throughout the countryside in Cuba. These *escuelas en el campo* have been a most creative innovation, contributing at one and the same time to integration of education and work, levelling out social distinctions within and between the rural and urban population and promoting ethnic harmony, agricultural development and self-reliance in education.

Major advances have also been made in the field of social security. Prior to the revolution some 30 per cent of the workforce was covered by social security legislation, but a series of measures taken since the early 1960s brought about a radical overhaul of the system and increased the coverage to practically all workers including private farmers. In the case of wage workers, coverage includes payments in case of illness, permanent disability and maternity leave and pensions on retirement. Cooperative farmers also enjoy the same protection, but the benefits are somewhat less. More recently, schemes have been developed to provide illness and disability benefits to private farmers and alternatives to retirement benefits have been worked out through the leasing or sale of land to the government.

It is generally recognised that progress has been much slower in the provision of adequate housing to the population. Although housing is a small financial burden on households, most of whom own their homes, there continues to be scarcity of good housing in urban areas and the quality of housing in rural areas is often extremely modest.

These then have been the principal social achievements of the revolution. The main policies and mechanisms which have facilitated such progress may be grouped under five heads: social ownership of the means of production, virtual elimination of open unemployment, provision of social consumption, structure of consumer prices and the system of food rationing.

Starting with the agrarian reform of 1959, public ownership of the economy was extended rapidly until by 1968 all sectors except agriculture were virtually entirely socialised. This, in effect, eliminated returns from capital as a source of income although many previous owners continued to receive some income as compensation for the takeover of their assets. Since income from property is generally the main source of inequality, the socialisation of the means of production contributed powerfully to income redistribution in favour of the erstwhile poverty groups. The egalitarian impact of this measure was further reinforced by the salary reform of 1962 under which the ratio between the lowest and the highest wage rates was reduced to 1:5.5.

The second element in improved income distribution was the virtual elimination of open unemployment. This contributed in three ways to a more even income distribution: absorption of the hard-core unemployed into regular employment, the extension of year-round employment to those who previously could get jobs only for a few months at the harvest time; and the entitlement of both these groups to benefits including social security accorded normally only to full-time employees. Since unemployment and underemployment constituted the core of the poverty problem in pre-revolutionary Cuba, the generation of full employment was a key element in the reduction and evential elimination of absolute poverty.

The structure of consumer prices has added further to the egalitarian thrust of government policies. In general, the prices of basic goods and services are kept relatively low while luxury and semi-luxury goods are priced relatively high. Among the former might be mentioned food staples, public transport, house rents, newspapers, books and recreational facilities. The latter would include alcohol, washing machines, television, refrigerators and above all automobiles. This point may be illustrated by the fact that the cost of a household food ration, which provides some 83 per cent of FAO's minimum calorie requirements, only requires 24 per cent of the minimum household income (i.e. the equivalent of two minimum wages). On the other hand, a refrigerator sold at *mercado paralelo* (parallel market) prices may amount to five to six months of the salary of a lower paid worker.

7.4 SOME DISTINCTIVE FEATURES OF CUBAN DEVELOPMENT STRATEGY

How has Cuba succeeded in combining relatively high economic growth with the mass provision of extensive social and welfare services? The key factors have been a high rate of accumulation, financed in part by internal savings in the form of surpluses by state enterprises and to an important degree by external grants, loans and assistance in kind; the priority given to productive investment in agriculture and industry and to upgrading of technical and professional skills; concentration of resources on meeting the basic needs of the masses and a tight squeeze on luxury expenditure. Some of these points are elaborated below.

The development strategy pursued by Cuba shares some common elements with other socialist countries, but there are also significant differences. Well before the end of the first decade after the revolution, the state had acquired all the means of production throughout the economy except for the agricultural sector. In the agricultural sector, the two agrarian reforms transferred large private estates and holdings to the state, but they also created a peasantry from the erstwhile tenants, sharecroppers and agricultural workers. Although the State was convinced of the superiority of socialist organisation in agriculture and was committed to achieving it, it did not resort to any coercive or hasty measures to bring this about.

Although the size of the private farm sector has declined over the years through deaths, retirements and voluntary sales of land to the State, a significant peasantry continued throughout the period to be an integral part of the Cuban economy and society. It was not until the mid-1970s that a decision was taken to give priority to production cooperatives and encourage private farmers to join them. It is likely that over the next decade the peasantry will gradually disappear through absorption of its land in cooperatives or state farms. But the policy to create and sustain a peasantry for over two decades remains a distinctive feature of Cuban development experience.

The second notable feature concerns the priority accorded to the agricultural sector. Except for the first two years of the revolution, this has been a constant of Cuban development policy and is manifested in allocation of investment funds and expenditure on infrastructure and social services. It is also reflected in the favourable treatment given to private farmers in contrast to the more usual policy of squeezing the agricultural sector and private farming in particular. Within the agricultural sector the decision was taken to emphasise the development of the sugar industry. In other words, the revolutionary Government opted for a development pattern based on traditional comparative advantage.

Several sympathetic observers of the Cuban scene have been critical of the priority given to agriculture over industry or of the emphasis placed on sugar rather than food production in agriculture. It has also been argued that because of its emphasis on agriculture and sugar, the Cuban economy failed to achieve structural change. It appears rather that given the resource endowments of the country, the external situation the country was faced with and the emphasis of the revolution on equality and elimination of poverty, the rural and agricultural bias was the appropriate one. The strategy of relying on sugar exports to pay for imports of food, raw materials and machinery appears also to have been the correct one, given the special trading arrangements with the USSR and other socialist countries. The USSR offered a steady and expanding market for sugar exports at stable prices several times world prices. At the same time, the agricultural sector and particularly the sugar industry has been massively modernised and mechanised and has developed extensive backward and forward linkages with other sectors of the economy.

The third striking feature of the Cuban development strategy has been the stress laid on development of human resources. At the outset, the Government mobilised the nation's entire resources for an assault on adult illiteracy. The following years saw a steady improvement in health facilities, educational opportunities and training in technical and vocational skills. The skill profile of the Cuban labour force has been transformed over the past two and a half decades and is no doubt an important factor in the acceleration of growth in the 1970s. The emphasis on human resources development, together with the expansion in employment opportunities, has also contributed to a sustained decline in birth rates and hence to a slow-down in the rate of population growth.

The fourth distinctive feature of the Cuban development policy has been reform within the socialist framework. The important reorientation in economic policies initiated in the 1970s, to reverse the pattern of slow growth, comprised a series of far-reaching changes accommodated within the framework of a socialist economy. This is the case, for example, with respect to wage and price reforms, use of economic accounting at the enterprise level, reliance on material incentives and decentralisation in management and decision-making. Indeed, in the rural sector, the socialist orientation of the development strategy was reinforced by the rapid expansion of production cooperatives and the use of land for *autoconsumo* on state farms and cooperatives. The latter may be regarded as an ingenious socialist solution to the problem of personal plots and the land allocated for *autoconsumo* may be described as collective 'personal' plots.

Finally, it is necessary to highlight the critical importance of the economic relationships with the USSR. The benefits to Cuba have accrued from favourable prices for its two main exports – sugar and nickel – and for its main import – oil; from the resale of unused oil; from grants and loans and from technical cooperation. Although there are no generally accepted estimates of the total assistance received from the socialist countries, there is little doubt that the aid furnished by them, especially the USSR, has been very high and has played a critical role in Cuban achievements in economic growth and social justice. It should be noted that Cuba has used the aid purposefully to strengthen her social and economic system and that the dedication, commitment and pragmatism of the Cuban leadership has played no small part in these achievements.

7.5 SOME UNDERLYING WEAKNESSES AND CRITICAL ISSUES

Despite considerable achievements in economic growth and social justice, the Cuban economy continues to suffer from some serious problems. These relate to weaknesses in some sectors and to efficiency in resource use.

A visitor to Cuba cannot but be struck by the inefficiency of some segments of the service sector, particularly retail trade, catering and repair services. These have been weak points of the economy for a long time. There is an urgent need for the expansion of these facilities and improvement in the quality of service.

Related to this is the continuance of the food rationing system and the limited availability, high cost and often poor quality of many consumer goods. In the early years of the revolution, the Cuban State rightly gave priority to achieving high growth and to meeting the essential needs of the population in education, health, food and clothing. But with the elimination of absolute poverty and the provision of basic health and educational services, Cuban society is demanding a wider range of consumer goods of good quality. In any case, these will be needed for the success of the policy of reliance on material incentives as a spur to efficiency and growth. The system of production and distribution has so far been insufficiently responsive to consumer preferences in terms of the quality and diversity of consumer goods. It will be necessary to continue experimenting and innovating to bring a greater coherence between the patterns of production and consumption.

The provision of a wider range and improved quality of goods and services will also require continuing increases in productivity and efficiency in resource use. This brings us to the question of the progress made in implementing the new system of economic planning and management designed to promote these objectives. Although the decision to adopt the new system seems already to have justified itself in the positive results obtained so far, its full implementation will take time. In particular, it is not clear to what extent the producer prices reflect costs and whether costs reflect social scarcity. In the absence of a sound price system, the greater autonomy enjoyed by the enterprises is unlikely to result in optimal allocation of resources.

At the same time, it is not clear that the full implications of the new system have been grasped and accepted. At the moment the decision-making process still seems highly centralised. In the future a proper balance will need to be struck between the need to give scope to local initiative and enterprise on the one hand, and to preserve central decision-making on some crucial issues on the other. This in turn raises the central question of worker participation in planning and decision-making at the enterprise level. Effective worker participation would seem essential to humanise the production process, to improve efficiency and to make it responsive to common needs.

At another level, decisions may need to be taken about the priority to be given to alternative methods of agricultural production, in particular state farms and cooperatives. In the past, the Cuban leadership has expressed a preference for state farms as a superior form of organisation, but cooperatives are a superior mechanism for worker participation in management. In any case, it appears that both these forms have distinctive strengths and the system may be able to get the best from mutual interaction and stimulation between them.

7.6 TOWARDS THE FUTURE

More than a quarter of a century has now elapsed since the agrarian reform was launched, and it can fairly be said that the very face of the Cuban countryside has been altered almost beyond recognition. The well-dressed, healthy youngsters in even the most remote rural areas perhaps best symbolise the striking contrast with pre-revolutionary Cuba, which these changes have produced.

Has rural Cuba then reached some kind of definition? It would surely be unrealistic to suppose that the changes of the next quarter-century of rural development can compare to the sweeping upheavals of the past twenty-five years. It seems fair to anticipate, for instance, that continuing mechanisation and investment will enable agriculture in general to increase and diversify its output as it has already been doing for some time.

Yet many effects of the changes that have already taken place have still to be fully felt. The massively enhanced social mobility of the rural population, for example, seems destined further to transform rural culture and lifestyles as a generation emerges whose roots are no longer deeply embedded in the soil. The decline of the small private farms already being experienced is only one aspect of this process.

The national economic position, too, is pregnant with uncertainty, especially as regards the country's balance of convertible currency. Sharply deteriorating terms of trade in the 1980s have elevated the island's hard cash debts of around US$3.5 thousand million from a side-issue to a serious obstacle to the fulfilment of economic programmes, demanding difficult annual renegotiations since 1982. Again, the future implications for rural Cuba are hard to calculate.

In this book, two policy developments of the past fifteen years have emerged as central themes; they are the rise of the cooperative farms to predominance within the non-state sector of agriculture, and the implantation of the Economic Planning and Management System (SDPE). Beyond their intrinsic significance, each, in its way, embodies the political and economic values that have characterised the recent period, with its emphasis on material motivation and greater scope for direct self-management.

Coinciding with the final preparation of this publication, in mid-1986, a 'revolutionary counter-offensive' was proclaimed by the political leadership,[1] against what was said to be widespread corruption, waste and inefficiency. The resonance with the 'revolutionary offensive' of the late 1960s is hardly coincidental, for once again the emphasis is swinging away from material incentives – without, however, this time threatening to abolish them altogether – to morality and revolutionary consciousness as the mainspring of national advancement.[2] No accident was it either that the planning system and the cooperatives emerged as particular objects of official scrutiny: the former for its inefficiency and mishandling of material inducements, and the latter for their alleged corruption and specifically the abuse of generous state credits for building materials.[3]

No one can predict how the future of rural Cuba will unfold, even if its main features are now in place. But it is not too early to say that rural labour and development in Cuba will continue to repay close attention and interest.

NOTES AND REFERENCES

1. Fidel Castro: speech to managers of Havana enterprises, in *Granma Semanal*, 8 July 1986, pp. 2–3.
2. Fidel Castro: speech to Cuba National Assembly, in *Granma Semanal*, 13 July 1986.
3. Fidel Castro: speech to agricultural production cooperatives, in *Granma Semanal*, 1 June 1986.

Glossary

Acopio: 'Collection' – the state procurement network for agricultural supplies. The term also covers the pricing system and other features of the procurement system.

'Administration cane': Sugar cane grown under direct management on company lands (see *colonos*).

Agromercados: State-run fruit and vegetable markets within the 'parallel market' system.

Alzadoras: Grab-lifters for loading cane on to the mill transport.

ANAP: The National Small Farmers' Association (*Asociación Nacional de Agricultores Pequeños*).

Anticipo: The share of a cooperatives' income paid to its members, the equivalent of wages.

Arrendatarios: Tenant farmers.

Asociaciones campesinas: Peasant associations – the generic label attached to the various forms of mutualism and self-help among individual private farmers.

Autoconsumo: 'Self-provisioning' – farm production on a state farm or cooperative for the consumption of the workers themselves and their families.

Batey: The town surrounding a sugar mill.

BEP: Special Production Brigade (*Brigada Especial de Producción*) – an integrated and largely self-managing work team in industry.

BPP: Permanent Production Brigade (*Brigada Permanente de Producción*) – an integrated and largely self-managing work team in agriculture.

Caballería: A traditional Spanish measurement of area still widely used in Cuba. One *caballería* equals approximately 13.5 hectares.

CAI: Agro-Industrial Complex (*Complejo Agro-Industrial*) – the CAIs are state enterprises responsible for all stages of sugar production, but the model is now being extended to other areas of agriculture.

CCS: Service and Credit Cooperative (*Cooperativa de Créditos y Servicios*).

Centavo: One-hundreth of a *peso*.

Cifras de control/cifras directivas: see Control Figures/Directed Figures.

Coeficientes de interés socio-económico: 'Coefficients of economic and social interest' – premiums paid for work of a particularly arduous/hazardous or economically important nature.

Colonos: Tenant farmers on company-owned sugar estates.

Cooperativas Cañeras: Cane Cooperatives – the first coops/state farms formed in the agrarian reform, subsequently converted into fully fledged state Sugar Farms (*Granjas Cañeras*) and finally Agro-Industrial Complexes (CAIs).

'Conditions': Criteria to be set for the distribution of *Primas and Premios*.

'Control Figures': The specific targets within a Control Plan.

'Control Plan': *Plan de Control* – the planning targets put forward by the state to the producers at the outset of the planning process.

Cooperativista: Member of a cooperative, usually a CPA.

'Cost per unit of production': A measure of profitability indicating the cost in inputs of producing one *peso* worth of output. Anything less than 1 *peso* implies a net gain.

CPA: Agricultural Production Cooperative (*Cooperativa de producción agropecuaria*) – today the dominant model in the non-state farming sector.

Dirección de Trabajo: The labour office run in each municipality by the People's Power authorities, whose responsibility is to coordinate employment in local areas, in close collaboration with the State Committee on Labour (*Comité Estatal de Trabajo*) and the local enterprises.

'Directed Plan': *Plan directiva* – the binding contract reached between producers and the State in the final stage of the planning process.

Fincas de Administración Directa: Direct Administration Farms – a transitional name applied to cattle ranches taken over by INRA during the agrarian reform.

Granjas Cañeras: Sugar Farms – state farms in the sugar sector, which have now been absorbed by the Agro-Industrial Complexes (CAIs).

Granjas del Pueblo: People's Farms – the formal title for state farms except in the sugar sector (see *Granjas Cañeras*).

Guajiro: Traditional name for the Cuban peasant.

Horario de conciencia: 'Conscience time' – an experiment of the late 1960s in which workers' attendance was subject only to moral constraints.

'Indicators': Criteria to be met for the distribution of *Primas* and *Premios*.

INRA: The National Agrarian Reform Institute (1965–76).

JUCEPLAN: The Central Planning Board (*Junta Central de Planificación*) – the body, with ministerial status, in charge of administering the central planning system (SDPE).

Libreta: The ration book.

Mercados campesinos: the now defunct small farmers' markets.

MINAG: Ministry of Agriculture.

MINAZ: Ministry of Sugar.

MINBAS: Ministry of Basic (or Heavy Industry).

MINIL: Ministry of Light Industry.

Partidarios: Sharecroppers.

PCC: The Communist Party of Cuba (*Partido Comunista de Cuba*).

Peso: The Cuban currency. Because it is non-convertible all attempts to calculate equivalents must be treated with caution. On the official exchange rate, US$1 has stood at around 0.89 *pesos* in recent years. For purposes of comparison it is often useful to remember that the average wage is around 170 *pesos* a month.

Plan de Control/Plan directiva: See Control Plan/Directed Plan.

Plantilla: The workforce of an enterprise, whose total size and detailed composition are agreed between the enterprise and the planning authorities. State enterprises are not permitted to exceed the specifications of their assigned *plantilla* without approval.

Poder Popular: 'People's Power' – the Cuban system of elective national, provincial and municipal government, founded in 1976. Delegates are elected in secret ballot at municipal level, and the provincial assemblies and the National Assembly are in turn elected by the delegates at the immediately inferior level. The People's Power National Assembly, or Parliament, meets twice yearly in sessions lasting three days. Delegates at all levels can be recalled at any time by these.

Precaristas: Squatters.

Premios: 'Prizes' – bonuses for workers distributed on the basis of collective performance. Management are eligible.

Primas: 'Awards' – bonuses for workers on the basis of individual performance. Management are ineligible.

SDPE: The Economic Management and Planning System (*Sistema de Dirección y Planificación Económica*).

Sociedades Agropecuarias: Agriculture and Livestock Societies – peasant cooperatives that formed largely spontaneously during the agrarian reform.

Subarrendatarios: Sub-tenant farmers.

Tiempo muerto: 'Dead time' – the months outside the harvest season when sugar workers traditionally experienced mass unemployment.

UJC: The Young Communist League (*Union de Jóvenes Comunistas*).

Venta Libre: 'Free sale' – goods that may be bought outside the ration system.

Vocales: 'Spokesmen/women' – general members of the management of a cooperative who do not have specific responsibilities.

Voluntaridad: 'Voluntariety' – the principle proclaimed in the Second Agrarian Reform of 1963 that henceforth private farmlands would only be taken over by the State with the consent of the owner. The same principle applies to joining a cooperative.

Zafra: The sugar harvest.

Index